ME?
OBEY
HIM?

ME?
OBEY
HIM?

The Obedient Wife and
God's Way of Happiness and
Blessing in the Home

By Elizabeth Rice Handford

SWORD of the LORD PUBLISHERS

P. O. Box 1099 • Murfreesboro, TN 37133
(800) 247-9673 (615) 893-6700 FAX (615) 848-6943
E-mail: 102657.3622@compuserve.com

Contents

Me? Obey Him?
Revised, Enlarged Edition

"I hated your book," a woman said to me, with tears in her eyes, "and I owe you an apology. Someone gave *Me? Obey Him?* to me because my marriage had gone sour. I read the first chapter and got so angry I tried to flush the book down the toilet. But it wouldn't go down. I tried to burn it, but the pages were too soggy. So I threw it across the living room. It hit the wall and landed on the floor—it lay there for weeks. All the while my relationship with my husband got worse.

"In desperation I picked up your book and read it through—this time with tears of shame—and hope. I put the Bible principles to work in my life; and oh, Libby, I can't thank you enough. My husband has come to Christ, and our home is happier than we could ever have imagined."

. . . . . .

I'm often asked, since I wrote this book in 1972, "Do you still believe what you wrote back then, or have times changed?"

The question ought not to be, "Do I still believe it?" but "What does God's Word say?"

Yes, I still believe God commands a woman to obey

her husband. This revised edition does not alter the message; it only relates it to the problems Christian women face in the twenty-first century. Chapter 7 is added to help you in appealing a poor decision.

As I've reread this book, I've exulted to see how the real women whose stories are narrated here have prospered in the intervening years. The child who wasn't aborted is now a strapping college senior, majoring in science, serving God and giving his parents unalloyed joy. The woman who decided she'd pick up her husband's clothes without murmuring is now a contented grandmother, thoroughly enjoying a second honeymoon with her husband in their empty nest. The unbelieving husband came to Christ, and he and his wife have served the Lord faithfully for these years.

And I—? Well, yes, a few times in these wonderful and fruitful intervening years, I have had to "walk like I talk" in *Me? Obey Him?*

I remember a balmy evening watching the teenage boys whip up and down the church parking lot on their skateboards. "I've always wanted to try that," I said. A kid grinned and pushed his board over to me. I put one foot on it, and the board shot out from under me like a bullet.

"Okay, guys, you're going to have to hold me up until I get the hang of it," I said, when a quiet, stern voice behind me said, "Libby, no!" (Please don't take my husband's side and say a woman in her sixties doesn't belong on a skateboard because she might break a hip!)

There was a long pause while I got my spirit under control, because I really did want to try it. But I was glad I'd responded well when I turned around and saw the mothers of those teenagers watching me with eyes wide to see if I would act like I'd taught them!

I remember climbing up into our airplane one drizzly winter night, determined to obey my husband, but very fearful because the weather forecast predicted freezing temperatures aloft. That flight did terminate safely, back at the airport we'd left from, after a thirty-minute, heart-stopping flight with the wings and prop dangerously iced and navigational radios too rimed to give dependable guidance.

So, yes, I've obeyed sometimes when I felt my husband was making an unwise decision. But that has been a rare experience, and as often as not, probably, he was right—and, oh, how God has been with us through forty-six years of marriage! How He has taken our imperfections—Walt's and mine—and led us safely day by day.

So, dear friend, please read the book all the way through, won't you, before you try to flush it down the toilet? You, too, may find it the best thing that ever happened to your marriage.

With love,

Elizabeth Handford

Summer, 1994
Shiloh on Shannon

Introduction

I am the "him" about whom Elizabeth Handford is speaking. With forty-six years of watching her life as a dedicated pastor's wife and successful mother of seven children, I can say Libby "practices what she preaches." She is the most unselfish person I know. She has deep, abiding, biblical convictions and never steps over the line of respect for the authority of her husband. Not always has she agreed with me in everything, but she has never "bucked" any decision I have made. She has followed me, painfully sometimes, through my changing enthusiasms—whether the farm, photography, flying, and now computers.

Libby works hard from early morning until late at night to carry out her duties as wife, mother, author, Sunday school teacher, and counselor to women on every kind of subject—from baby-care to marriage-saving. The message in *Me? Obey Him?* is not theory but advice forged on the anvil of years of experience. I have seen strong-willed, nagging wives changed into sweet, submissive mates after counseling with her. Homes are back together because her wise advice was heeded. The work of God has been advanced because Libby has helped the wives of Christian workers to become partners rather than opponents of their husbands.

The strong Bible message on a good wife's position

of submissiveness is especially needed today when women's lib and unisex have had such a devastating impact. Unless our homes can return to the principles given in this book, America cannot long continue any kind of a moral society.

Read this book with your heart open and share its message with others. "Me" and "him" will be grateful.

Dr. Walter Handford, Pastor
Southside Baptist Church
Greenville, South Carolina

Summer, 1994

First, a Favor, Please

Some of the ideas in these pages may be absolutely new to you and foreign to everything you have ever believed. Hopefully, you will find them absolutely faithful to the Scriptures and they will lead to holy and happy living. Because this is an area fraught with opinion and prejudice, you'll need to ask the Lord to open your heart and mind to the truth. Ask Him to show you exactly what He requires. Then, if I touch a place of need in your life, you will recognize it and seek cleansing for it.

John 7:17 says, "If any man will do his will, he shall know of the doctrine, whether it be of God, or whether I speak of myself." If you are willing to do what God shows you, then you can know what He wants you to do. Are you willing to do whatever He says? Really willing? Without any reservations or "buts"? If God will make His will absolutely plain to you, will you do it? The Scripture says you can know the Bible teaching concerning a wife's subjection to her husband and enter into the blessed fulfillment of your womanhood.

1

Why Did God Command a Wife to Obey Her Husband?

The dew still sparkled on God's new creation when He looked down on a lonely Adam. "It is not good," He said, "that the man should be alone; I will make him an help meet for him" (Gen. 2:18). God then fashioned every beast of the field and every fowl of the air and brought them to Adam. Adam delighted in them and called them all by name. He saw the lion play with his lioness, the bear cavort with his mate. All the creatures of the new world seemed to have a companion just fitted for them. But for Adam there was not found an helpmeet.

So God caused a deep sleep to fall on Adam, and from Adam's body God took a rib and made a woman. In the breaking of that manly body, in the shedding of Adam's blood, the sundering of bone and flesh, Eve found life. And only she, of all the creatures of the earth, met the needs of Adam's body, of his heart and mind. She was a help "meet" for him, suited for him in every way.

God could have created Eve from the dust of the

ground, as He created Adam, but He chose not to. It seems He wanted Adam to know how greatly he needed Eve, wanted him to understand she was actually a part of his body, as intimate a part as hand or foot. He must have wanted Adam and Eve to understand they were actually physically one flesh in the deepest and holiest sense of the word. And that miracle of oneness is created again even today when a man and woman stand before God, take one another, forsaking all others, and become one flesh.

That day, in the unspoiled Garden of Eden, God established the single most important relationship a human being can ever enter into with another human being. He gave man a woman, to be companion, friend, compassionate helpmeet, lover, and heir with him in the grace of creating new life.

But one dark day—the darkest day in all the world, darker even than the day Christ gave His life on the cross, because this day made necessary that day—Eve listened to the serpent in the garden. She believed Satan's lie. She touched the forbidden fruit, plucked it, tasted it, and gave it to her husband. Together they inherited, not the God-likeness Satan had promised, but the curse of death.

When God walked through the garden in the cool of that somber day, He found His two creatures hiding, shivering in the nakedness of their sin. In a voice that struck dread in the heart of that first woman, God said to her, "Thy desire shall be to thy husband, and he shall rule over thee" (Gen. 3:16).

Then that great God of Heaven and earth, holy

beyond our comprehension and loving beyond all understanding, stooped to earth and fashioned for them coverings of skin by the shedding of blood. He is infinitely holy. He is infinitely loving. He joined these two unalterable attributes to make salvation possible for the sinning children of His creation.

The command uttered that day to the stricken wife still stands: "Thy desire shall be to thy husband, and he shall rule over thee."

There are three major reasons for the command. And because the *why* of the command makes the *what* of the command more bearable, let's think first about why God requires a wife to obey her husband.

Makes it bearable? There! It slipped out! Alas, fellow-women, I confess that obedience even to a really good man isn't easy, and sometimes it's nearly intolerable! That much I admit—but stick with me for awhile, won't you?

God's Perfect Creation Required Order

Even in the Garden of Eden, before the sin of Adam and Eve, God had set up the chain of command. It required the husband to be in authority over the woman. First Timothy 2:11–13 says, "Let the woman learn in silence with all subjection. But I suffer not a woman to . . . usurp authority over the man, but to be in silence. For [because] Adam was first formed, then Eve."

In human enterprise of any kind, leadership is required. Someone has to be in charge. But no one, no matter how much authority he has, operates without restraints over him. A husband has authority over his wife. But that husband has many authorities he must answer to: civil law, economic realities, social conscience. Even if he is his own boss, he has constraints upon him. Even God's perfect creation required order.

First Corinthians 11:3 gives the chain of command: "But I would have you know, that the head of every man is Christ; and the head of the woman is the man; and the head of Christ is God."

There is an order of authority in the universe, and it is set up like this:

Christ

Man

Woman

The first surprise in the chain of command is that Christ is subject to God the Father. He is equal with God, is very God, but He is subject to the Father. In the Garden of Gethsemane He prayed, "O my Father...not as I will, but as thou wilt" (Matt. 26:39). Hebrews 5:8 says, "Though he were a Son, yet learned he obedience by the things which he suffered."

"I seek not mine own will," Jesus said in John 5:30, "but the will of the Father which hath sent me." Philippians 2:5–8 says that, though He was God Himself, He took the form of a servant, and humbled Himself, became obedient to death, even the death of the cross. Even when Christ has conquered all the forces of evil, I Corinthians 15:28 says He will submit Himself to God: "And when all things shall be subdued unto him, then shall the Son also himself be subject unto him that put all things under him, that God may be all in all." Jesus, the Creator of Heaven and earth, submitted Himself to God the Father. He took His place in the chain of command.

It is no shame, no dishonor, for a woman to be under authority, if the Lord Jesus—very God Himself— submitted to the authority of the Father.

Position in the chain of authority has nothing to do with the individual's worth to God or value to others. It does not determine one's importance. A woman is subject to her husband, but she can still go directly to God, to ask anything she needs or desires, and get it as quickly as if she were a man. Galatians 3:28 says, "There is neither Jew nor Greek, there is neither bond nor free, there is neither male nor female: for ye are all one in Christ Jesus."

God is not a respecter of persons. Whoever "feareth him, and worketh righteousness, is accepted with him" (Acts 10:34, 35). God hears the prayers of a godly woman just as quickly as He hears the prayers of a godly man.

Nor should a man be "puffed up" because he stands above the woman in the chain of command. Paul explains it in I Corinthians 11:7-12: "For a man indeed ought not to cover his head, forasmuch as he is the image and glory of God: but the woman is the glory of the man. For the man is not of the woman; but the woman of the man. Neither was the man created for the woman; but the woman for the man. . . . Nevertheless [lest a husband should strut himself unduly] neither is the man without the woman, neither the woman without the man, in the Lord. For as the woman is of the man, even so is the man also by the woman; but all things of God." There is no place for boasting, by man or woman, and no need for chafing as if woman had an inferior position.

Each has a blessed, unique responsibility, a purpose in life that the other cannot possibly fulfill and cannot happily exist without.

God made the man to be the achiever, the doer, to provide for the home and protect it, to be high priest and intercessor for the home. His body carries the seed of life, and he is responsible for the children that will be born, to guide them, nurture them, direct them.

God made the woman to be a keeper of the home, to make a haven within its walls, a retreat from the stress of battle for every member of the family, the nourisher of the children. A woman's body is fashioned for being a wife and mother. (Why, oh why, should a feminist think that's degrading?) Her body is shaped for the bearing of children, and never a month goes by but what she is reminded of the basic, creative function of motherhood. All the sense of her being answers to the wail of a baby, to the uplifted arms of a child. (Have you ever wondered what caused the pampered daughter of Pharaoh to adopt the infant of the despised children of Israel? "She saw the child: and, behold, the babe wept. And she had compassion on him" [Exod. 2:6]. The need of the weeping baby Moses overcame all the conditioning and training she had received!)

A woman is different from a man. (I know that sounds like a stupid statement. But if you have read some of the writers of the current women's lib movement, you'll realize they don't believe it. They think a woman is different only because she has been conditioned to inferiority from babyhood, and exploited by it!) A woman is different in her body, in her interests, in her thinking, in her abilities: not inferior—different.

Women have entered the marketplace. They have achieved fame in medicine, in business, in the arts. A woman can choose nearly any occupation she likes, and God values her for herself, whatever occupation she chooses, for it is not His will that every woman marry (Matt. 19:12; Isa. 56:3–5). But her fulfillment, in the will of God for her life, will not surpass that which a godly Christian woman, also in the will of God, finds who, secure in the knowledge of her womanhood and its rightness, builds a home for her husband and children! Her confidence in her ability to be a helpmeet, sufficient for her husband's needs, comes as she finds her place in the order of authority.

Woman's Nature Requires Her Obedience

The second reason God requires a woman to be subject to her husband is also found in I Timothy 2:11–15. This reason is not easy to accept, and yet it is a part of finding peace in the home. "Let the woman learn in silence with all subjection. But I suffer not a woman to . . . usurp authority over the man . . . . Adam was not deceived, but the woman being deceived was in the transgression. Notwithstanding she shall be saved in childbearing, if they continue in faith and charity and holiness with sobriety."

The command in Genesis 3:16 was given in direct consequence of Eve's sin. She was the one who "saw that the tree was good for food, and that it was pleasant to the eyes, and a tree to be desired to make one wise." She was the one who "took of the fruit thereof, and did eat, and gave also unto her husband with her." Eve was deceived; Adam was not. He knew the consequences of eating the forbidden fruit. She did not.

(How fraught with meaning is that picture of the first Adam, eating of the forbidden fruit for the sake of his beloved wife, knowing he ate of death! He foreshadows the second Adam, Christ, who knew no sin, but was made sin for us, so we could have salvation—II Cor. 5:21.)

We perhaps have the impression that women as a class are more spiritually minded than men, with sensibilities more refined, and purer thoughts. It hurts my feminine pride to have to admit that is not necessarily true! A woman may be more susceptible to spiritual error than a man because of her intuitive, emotional thinking. Intuitive thinking is God's gift, and infinitely valuable, but it needs the balance of reason. I should add, too, that a woman does not have to be led into error. That is one reason God commanded her not to usurp authority over the man, so she can be protected from false doctrine.

A wife who rejects authority leaves herself open to every false teacher who will "creep into houses, and lead captive silly women laden with sins, led away with divers lusts, Ever learning, and never able to come to the knowledge of the truth" (II Tim. 3:6, 7).

Jeremiah, chapter 44, tells the incomprehensible story of Israelites down in Egypt. A pitiful remnant had run from Jerusalem, dragging the Prophet Jeremiah with them. "Jeremiah," the men cried, "tell us the word of God. Whatever you tell us He says, we will obey." So Jeremiah said, "All right, God says destroy your idols and turn back to God with all your hearts." Then verses 15 and 16 say: "Then all the men which *knew that their wives had burned incense unto other gods,* and all the women that stood by, a great multitude, even all the people that dwelt in the land of Egypt, in Pathros, answered Jeremiah, saying, As for the word that thou hast spoken unto us in the name of the Lord, we will not hearken unto thee." The women seized the spiritual leadership. They led the men into idolatry.

When a woman usurps the spiritual leadership of the home, it always leads to tragedy. Sarah thought she had a solution to what was basically a spiritual problem —her barrenness. God had already promised her a son, but she got impatient and unbelieving. She suggested Abraham take Hagar, her maid. The child of that union, Ishmael, brought estrangement and heartache, and millenniums of conflict between Arab and Jew.

Genesis 27 tells the story of Rebekah's conspiracy against her aged, blind husband Isaac. She wanted her favorite, the younger son Jacob, to receive his patriarchal blessing. (How many lessons we could learn from that sad family relationship, when father and mother chose favorites and fostered jealousy between the children!) She went to great lengths to deceive him, and the woe that followed her deception can hardly be up: Esau's murderous hatred, Jacob's banishment for twenty-one toil-filled years. And all of it, *all* of it, was unnecessary because God Himself had promised Rebekah, before the twins were born, that "the elder shall serve the younger" (Gen. 25:23). When that poor wife started managing (and muddling) the spiritual affairs of her home, she snarled all the good things God intended to accomplish in His own good time.

Yet another illustration of this is found in Exodus, chapter 4. Moses, saved from death by his mother's faith, rejecting the splendor of Pharaoh's court, mistaking the way to redeem his people from their bondage, fled to the wilderness. During his forty years of exile, he married Zipporah, an Ethiopian, daughter of the priest of Midian. Two sons were born to them.

Then Moses met God face to face. God commissioned him to give Pharaoh a message: "Israel is my first-born. Let him go free." Moses put his wife and sons on an ass and went back to Egypt to free his people. They stopped at an inn in Egypt for the night.

But what is this? A form wrestles with Moses and seeks to kill him. Who is it? The Lord! God Himself is trying to kill Moses! But why? Why would God try to kill the man He had just sent to redeem Israel? It is the child, Gershom. He is not circumcised! The sign of the covenant between Israel and God, commanded to be executed upon every son—Moses has broken the covenant! But he cannot save himself—God holds him in the grip of death, and Moses is helpless to correct his fault.

Zipporah seizes a sharp stone, circumcises the child, throws the foreskin down at Moses' feet. God is satisfied. Moses is released.

What does it all mean? How did Zipporah know what was needed? Zipporah was not a Jew, perhaps was not a believer. (Her father was not, until he saw the wonders God did in bringing Israel out of Egypt—Exod. 18:8–11.) How did she know why God was about to kill her husband? The clue is found in what she said to her husband: 'Thou art a bloody husband to me.' Evidently Moses had intended to circumcise the child, and Zipporah had protested that it was "too bloody." She evidently did not like the aesthetics of her husband's bloody religion. However, to save her husband's life, she would circumcise the child, but still in rebellion.

They did not continue the journey together. Aaron found Moses back at the Mount of God and went with him back to Egypt to accomplish his great task. Zipporah stayed in Midian with her father until after the children of Israel came out of Egypt.

By interfering with her husband's spiritual leadership in the home, she nearly caused his death. She lost all the reward of being a helpmeet to her husband (and how he must have needed it in those overwhelming days!) in the greatest crisis of his life. And, judging from the importance given it throughout Scripture, she missed being a part of one of the most glorious events in the history of mankind!

Consider the terrible results when the wife of a king sets out to manage the spiritual life of the home. King Solomon was "beloved of God," wonderfully endowed. He was the child of King David, whom God had promised would always have a son to sit on the throne of David. But Solomon's wives "turned away his heart after other gods." The supremely blessed Solomon, wiser than any other man, builder of the Temple of the most high God, stooped to building temples for the wicked idols of his wives (I Kings 11:1–13). The division of the kingdom and a thousand years of civil war were the terrible price paid

because one man let his wives assume the spiritual
leadership of the home!

A Wife's Submission Pictures the Submission of the Church to Christ

God expects a woman to obey her husband because
the husband-wife relationship pictures the holy, inef-
fably sweet relationship between Christ and His bride,
the people for whom He died. This is explained in Ephesians 5:22–33:

*"Wives, submit yourselves unto your own husbands,
as unto the Lord. For the husband is the head of the wife,
even as Christ is the head of the church: and he is the
saviour of the body. Therefore as the church is subject
unto Christ, so let the wives be to their own husbands
in every thing.*

*"Husbands, love your wives, even as Christ also loved
the church, and gave himself for it; That he might sanc-
tify and cleanse it with the washing of water by the word,
That he might present it to himself a glorious church,
not having spot, or wrinkle, or any such thing; but that
it should be holy and without blemish. So ought men to
love their wives as their own bodies. He that loveth his
wife loveth himself. For no man ever yet hated his own
flesh; but nourisheth and cherisheth it, even as the Lord
the church:*

*"For we are members of his body, of his flesh, and
of his bones. For this cause shall a man leave his father
and mother, and shall be joined unto his wife, and they
two shall be one flesh. This is a great mystery: but I speak
concerning Christ and the church. Nevertheless let every*

*one of you in particular so love his wife even as himself;
and the wife see that she reverence her husband."*

The Lord intends for marriage to be as delightful,
as sweet and intimate and tender as the relationship
He wants us to experience with Him. And, in turn, He
wants our fellowship with Him to be as real and tangible as that we have with our mate.

Christ's love for the church compelled Him to give
Himself for it. "While we were yet sinners," Romans
5:8 says, "Christ died for us." See the bedraggled, soiled
bride, cleansed and sanctified, dressed in the garments
of her bridegroom's righteousness, coming to her bridegroom's home, holy and without blemish!

Just as Adam's body was broken to give life to Eve,
so in a mystic, miraculous way, God makes the husband
the saviour of his wife's body. "For the husband is the
head of the wife...and he is the saviour of the body"
(Eph. 5:23). How? I cannot tell. Certainly physically he
is the saviour of his wife, as he defends her against tangible dangers; physically, too, as he assumes the burden
of providing her shelter, food, warmth, clothing; certainly emotionally, as his strong, manly confidence allays
her fears and uncertainties; and also, evidently—though
I cannot tell you just how—spiritually.

Ezekiel, chapter 16, tells the poignant story of One
who found a newborn baby girl lying in the field, wallow-
ing in her natal blood. He took that polluted body,
cleaned it and nourished it. He provided every need of
her childhood, and watched as she grew into young
womanhood. Then verse 8 says, "Now when I passed by
thee, and looked upon thee, behold, thy time was the

time of love; and I spread my skirt over thee, and covered thy nakedness: yea, I sware unto thee, and entered into a covenant with thee, saith the Lord God, and thou becamest mine." The husband takes his bride, and his garments cover her nakedness, spiritually as well as physically.

A wife is to obey her husband because she pictures the obedient bride of Christ, cleansed and ornamented, entering into the unspeakable joy of union with her Lord. How could that kind of obedience be onerous, a thing to be ashamed of, despised?

2

What Do the Scriptures Say About a Wife's Obedience?

We have found *why* God commands a wife's obedience. Now let's see *what* obedience the Scriptures require.

Genesis 3:16: "Unto the woman [God] said,...thy desire shall be to thy husband, and he shall rule over thee."

First Corinthians 11:3: "But I would have you know, that the head of every man is Christ; and the head of the woman is the man; and the head of Christ is God."

First Corinthians 11:8, 9: "For the man is not of the woman; but the woman of the man. Neither was the man created for the woman; but the woman for the man."

Ephesians 5:22: "Wives, submit yourselves unto your own husbands, as unto the Lord." (Living Letters paraphrases this: "Submit to your husband's leadership in the same way you submit to the Lord.")

Ephesians 5:24: "As the church is subject unto Christ, so let the wives be to their own husbands in every thing."

Ephesians 5:33: "Let...the wife see that she reverence [respect] her husband."

Colossians 3:18: "Wives, submit yourselves unto your own husbands, as it is fit in the Lord." (Living Letters: "You wives, submit yourselves to your husbands, for that is what the Lord has planned for you." Williams Translation: "for this is your Christian duty"; or, the footnote says, "literally 'fitting in the Lord'—that is, it is proper, or as it befits a Christian.")

Notice this Scripture says, "*as* it is fit," not "*if* it is fit."

First Timothy 2:11, 12: "Let the woman learn in silence with all subjection. But I suffer not a woman to teach, nor to usurp authority over the man, but to be in silence."

Titus 2:4, 5: The aged women, mature Christians, are to "teach the young women to be sober, to love their husbands, to love their children, To be discreet, chaste, keepers at home, good, obedient to their own husbands, that the word of God be not blasphemed." (Disobedient wives blaspheme the Word of God! Insubordination is as great a sin as cursing God!)

First Peter 3:1: "Likewise, ye wives, be in subjection to your own husbands; that, if any obey not the word, they also may without the word be won by the conversation [behavior] of the wives."

First Peter 3:5, 6: "For after this manner in the old time the holy women also, who trusted in God, adorned themselves, being in subjection unto their own husbands: Even as Sara obeyed Abraham, calling him lord:

whose daughters ye are, as long as ye do well, and are not afraid with any amazement."

There are many other Scriptures concerning obedience to authority; these specifically tell a wife to obey her husband.

Before we go any further, let's consider: regardless of your idea of what these Scriptures *mean*, can we agree that they all *say* a wife should obey her husband?

Beyond a shadow of a doubt, the Scriptures *say* a woman ought to obey her husband!

Why not reread each verse, answering these questions:

Is there, in any one of them, a restriction on a wife's obedience?

Does a single Scripture mention any situation where a wife ought not to obey?

Is any command qualified by any "if"? *if* the husband were not a Christian? *if* the wife thought God were leading her contrary to his command?

Is there a hint, in any Scripture, that a wife may have to choose between conflicting authorities?

If you are intellectually honest, you have to admit that it is impossible to find a single loophole, a single exception, an "if" or "unless." The Scriptures say, without qualification, to the open-minded reader, that a woman ought to obey her husband.

She Is to Obey Regardless of His Spiritual Condition

A wife obeys her husband whether he is a Christian

or not, whether he is spiritually minded or not, whether
he earns her respect or not. It is his position as head
of the wife that she honors, not his personality. In fact,
the contrary is true. A wife is to be especially obedient
if her husband is not saved, according to I Peter 3:1.

The wife who obeys her husband may win him by
her meek and quiet spirit, her loving behavior.

She Need Not Fear Conflicting Authority

There is no hint that a woman may have to choose
between conflicting authority. God knows it is impossible to live under two rulers. Jesus said in Matthew 6:24:
"No man can serve two masters: for either he will hate
the one, and love the other; or else he will hold to the
one, and despise the other. Ye cannot serve God and
mammon."

God commanded children to obey their parents.
Therefore God was especially careful that the child
grown to manhood understand he is released from the
authority of his parents when he marries. "Therefore
shall a man leave his father and his mother, and shall
cleave unto his wife" (Gen. 2:24). When a man marries,
he is freed from the authority of his parents and becomes
responsible directly to Christ.

Even so a woman is also released from her responsibility to her father when she marries. Numbers
30:3, 6, 16 shows plainly that a girl answers to her father
until she marries. Then she is free from the father's
authority and responsible to her husband. God does not
expect a woman to have to answer to conflicting
authorities.

Certainly she will be subject to other authorities.

Hebrews 13:17: "Obey them that have the rule over you, and submit yourselves: for they watch for your souls, as they that must give account."

Romans 13:1, 2: "Let every soul be subject unto the higher powers. For there is no power but of God: the powers that be are ordained of God. Whosoever therefore resisteth the power, resisteth the ordinance of God: and they that resist shall receive to themselves damnation."

First Peter 2:13–15: "Submit yourselves to every ordinance of man for the Lord's sake: whether it be to the king, as supreme; Or unto governors, as unto them that are sent by him for the punishment of evildoers, and for the praise of them that do well. For so is the will of God, that with well doing ye may put to silence the ignorance of foolish men."

Notice that here again obedience is required because of position, not because the individual merits it. Paul called Ananias a whited wall, but when he found out he was the high priest, he apologized: "I wist not, brethren, that he was the high priest: for it is written, Thou shalt not speak evil of the ruler of thy people" (Acts 23:3–5).

Sometimes the words of Peter and John in Acts 4:19, 20 are used as an excuse for not obeying authority. Peter and John had been commanded not to speak in the name of Jesus. They answered: "Whether it be right in the sight of God to hearken unto you more than unto God, judge ye. For we cannot but speak the things which we have seen and heard." In Acts 5:29 Peter said, "We ought to obey God rather than men."

These two Scriptures have often been used as an excuse for civil or wifely disobedience. But to do so misses the whole point. The result of the testimony was: "They let them go, finding nothing how they might punish them" (Acts 4:21). Why? Because they had not broken any laws, civil or religious!

There are some examples in the Bible of a Christian's breaking a civil law in order to keep God's law. They are extremely rare. And never did the civil authority suffer lack because a man obeyed God.

Daniel, long before he was put in the lions' den, proved his value to the kings of Babylon. So had Shadrach, Meshach, and Abed-nego, walking about in the flames of the fiery furnace.

Moses did not choose to suffer affliction with the people of God until "he was come to years"—that is, no longer responsible to Pharaoh's daughter. The civil government never suffers when a man of God obeys God. Rather, Jesus taught that a Christian ought to, and can, fulfill both obligations. "Render therefore unto Caesar the things which are Caesar's; and unto God the things that are God's" (Matt. 22:21).

Again, "Wherefore ye must needs be subject, not only for wrath, but also for conscience sake. For for this cause pay ye tribute also: for they are God's ministers, attending continually upon this very thing. Render therefore to all their dues: tribute to whom tribute is due; custom to whom custom; fear to whom fear; honor to whom honor" (Rom. 13:5–7).

If a miracle is needed in order for God's child to fulfill both obligations, God will do a miracle to make it possible. The tax collector came to Peter, asking for Jesus' taxes. Jesus told Peter that the children of the King didn't need to pay taxes ("Then are the children free..."). "Notwithstanding," He added, "lest we should offend them, go thou to the sea, and cast an hook, and take up the fish that first cometh up; and when thou hast opened his mouth, thou shalt find a piece of money: that take, and give unto them for me and thee" (Matt. 17:26, 27).

It is safe to conclude that when God told a woman to obey her husband, He intended for her to be able to do so without the risk of disobeying other authorities.

She Obeys Without Reference to Her Feelings About the Will of God

Suppose a woman feels God is leading her definitely opposite to what her husband insists she do. It's something not addressed in the Scriptures, not in the moral law of God, but she feels very strongly that God wants her to act contrary to what her husband demands. Whom should she obey? The Scriptures say a woman must ignore her "feelings" about the will of God, and do what her husband says. She can be certain of what God wants her to do, as if God had spoken audibly from Heaven!

I heard your gasp. It's hard to believe that the man you are married to, lovable and wonderful as he sometimes is, often grumpy and temperamental—it's hard to believe that man could be the actual voice of God in your life!

But listen to Numbers 30:6-16:

"And if she had at all an husband, when she vowed, or uttered ought out of her lips, wherewith she bound her soul; And her husband heard it, and held his peace at her in the day that he heard it: then her vows shall stand, and her bonds wherewith she bound her soul shall stand.

"But if her husband disallowed her on the day that he heard it; then he shall make her vow which she vowed, and that which she uttered with her lips, wherewith she bound her soul, of none effect: and the Lord shall forgive her. . . .

"And if she vowed in her husband's house, or bound her soul by a bond with an oath; And her husband heard it, and held his peace at her, and disallowed her not: then all her vows shall stand, and every bond wherewith she bound her soul shall stand.

"But if her husband hath utterly made them void on the day he heard them; then whatsoever proceeded out of her lips concerning her vows, or concerning the bond of her soul, shall not stand: her husband hath made them void; and the Lord shall forgive her. . . .

"But if he shall any ways make them void after that he hath heard them; then he shall bear her iniquity. These are the statutes, which the Lord commanded Moses, between a man and his wife."

This passage teaches two major truths: one, that a husband is given the right by God to prevent his wife from taking a spiritual step she feels led to take; and two, that if he does, God holds him accountable—"he shall bear her iniquity."

Here is a good woman who feels a burden to do a certain thing for God. She makes a vow to do so. In obedience to God's Word, she asks her husband's permission to do it. If her husband "disallows" it, if he will not permit her to do it, then God says she is free of her vow. Her husband is the one who will stand accountable to God for it. If it turns out that his decision is wrong, then he is the one who will bear the blame.

Why did God make this rule? Because it is a burden too heavy for a woman to bear, if she is required to assess every decision of her husband's to ascertain if it is really right or wrong. If she is forced to determine what is right, and act accordingly, then her behavior cannot be called obedience. She is making the final decision about what she will or will not do. God never intended for a woman to have to be accountable to Him for the rights or wrongs of her husband's decisions. If she does right consistently, then God will protect her from having to do something morally and irretrievably wrong.

Hannah's vow, in I Samuel 1, illustrates the practical working of this principle. Hannah promised God that, if He would give her a baby boy, she would give him back to Him. But it was not until Elkanah had approved the vow ("Do what seemeth thee good") that she was able to keep her vow.

It's important to see that this passage is talking about a definite act of worship, or dedication, which a woman wants to make. It concerns her doing a positive good. It does not mention anything about a husband's requiring a wife to break one of God's commands. Why not? Because God is not going to give anybody two conflicting commands so that it is impossible to obey them both!

⚮ 3 ⚮

Does God Really Mean What He Says?

We agreed, didn't we, that God's Word *says* a wife ought to obey her husband? We found the biblical reasons for the command. We could not find an exception when obedience might not be required, not one qualifying "if."

Still, if you are like me, something down inside says, "Yes, but surely sometimes there must be exceptions. Look, what if my husband commanded me to go murder somebody? Are you trying to tell me I ought to do it? What if my husband's command conflicts with God's commands?"

Isn't it strange that we choose this particular command of God to challenge? We could say the same thing about any two of the Ten Commandments, but we don't. We don't go around asking, "What should I do if I have to make a choice between murdering or stealing?" We don't lose any sleep at night worrying, "What if I have to choose between committing adultery or bearing false witness?"

Why not? Because the Scriptures and reason both tell us God would never give two orders impossible to obey. The single attribute of God the Scriptures most often tell us about is His perfect holiness, His absolute fairness, His unchanging righteousness. Psalm 145:17 says, "The Lord is righteous in all his ways, and holy in all his works." Would the God whose name is Holiness (Isa. 57:15)—would that God make it impossible for His children to keep His commandments, and then punish them for it? Certainly not! "Shall not the Judge of all the earth do right?" (Gen. 18:25).

Would a Loving, Righteous God Make It Impossible for a Woman to Do Right?

In Matthew 7:7-11, the Lord Jesus asked the question, 'If you had a little boy, and he asked you for a piece of bread, would you give him a rock? If he asked for an egg, would you give him a scorpion?'

The obvious answer is, "Of course not!" We might be frail, careless, unwise parents, but we would not deliberately play a dirty trick like that on a little child.

"Neither will your heavenly Father," Jesus answers. If you, being evil (a mortal, sinning human being) would not do that to your children, then realize your heavenly Father won't put you in that kind of bind either. He gives only good gifts to His children when they ask Him.

Psychologists say that schizophrenia (split personality) is sometimes caused by a parent who kept the child in a continual doublebind, by making contradictory rules impossible to keep. But normal fathers and mothers don't do that. However we fail in other ways, we don't intentionally give our children opposing commands. God is perfect; He wouldn't do it either. It is a slander against a holy, loving God to think He would give two commands impossible to keep.

Suppose a woman says, "Dear Lord, I really love You. With all my heart I want to serve You and do Your will. I read in Your Word that I'm supposed to obey You by obeying my husband, and that's what I'm going to do." Is it conceivable that our heavenly Father, righteous and loving as He certainly is, would give her the evil gift of making her sin? No, never. That is not the kind of God we serve! Our God commands, and then He makes it so we can obey. That is His eternal commitment to His children.

So relax, dear, perplexed child of God. Rest in the assurance that God will give you wisdom and ability to do His perfect will. You can obey your husband with all your heart and, obeying him, obey God!

However, the fact remains that sometimes a man forbids a woman to do something she thinks is commanded in Scripture. How can this be reconciled?

A Woman's Conscience Is Not a Safe Guide

It's important to remember that sometimes our sense of what is right and wrong can be distorted. Conscience is not a safe guide. Only the Scriptures, in their full meaning, are. I once knew a woman who took the Scripture in Proverbs 31:16 about the virtuous woman who "considereth a field, and buyeth it" as her justification for buying a lot for a new house when her husband told her not to. That Scripture simply is not giving a woman permission to go against her husband's will, whatever she wants to think.

Isaiah 44:20 describes a man in his worship who is so warped that he can't even realize he is lying to himself: "A deceived heart hath turned him aside, that he cannot deliver his soul, nor say, Is there not a lie in my right hand?"

Women led astray by false prophets cannot understand the truth: they are "Ever learning, and never able to come to the knowledge of the truth" (II Tim 3:6, 7).

Peter says that the Scriptures can be twisted (not necessarily intentionally) by the unlearned and unstable, to their own destruction (II Pet. 3:16).

"Feelings" about what is right and wrong are not dependable. What does the Word of God say, considered in its context?

There Are Priorities in Commandments

Some commandments are irrevocable, without exception. Some commandments have a qualification. *"If it be possible, as much as lieth in you,* live peaceably with all men" (Rom. 12:18) is an example. This is not a "situation ethics" idea, when people distort God's laws to feed their lusts.

But God often recognizes the fact that people cannot control the actions of others and therefore makes His commands accordingly.

We may not use the keeping of a lesser command as an excuse for breaking the greater command.

Timothy's mother Eunice was a believing Jew,

married to a Gentile, probably not a believer (Acts 16:1). Now God commanded that every Jewish baby boy be circumcised (Gen. 17:9–14). If he were not, the covenant would be broken and that soul cut off from his people. (You'll remember that God felt it was so important that He sought Moses' life because he had not circumcised his son.)

Nevertheless, Timothy was not circumcised. Why? Perhaps because his father did not permit it. Yet God honored the faith of Eunice and greatly used her son Timothy. The law of obedience to her husband superseded the law of circumcision. God held the father, not the mother, accountable.

Sometimes Bible characters tried to use a command of God to thwart His greater command. For example, King Saul brought cattle and sheep back from the battle with the Amalekites so he could make a sacrifice to God. Well, why wasn't it all right? Hadn't God commanded sacrifices? Yes, but not of the cattle God had said destroy! "Hath the Lord as great delight in burnt-offerings and sacrifices, as in obeying the voice of the Lord? Behold, to obey is better than sacrifice, and to hearken than the fat of rams. For rebellion is as the sin of witchcraft, and stubbornness is as iniquity and idolatry. Because thou hast rejected the word of the Lord, he hath also rejected thee from being king" (I Sam. 15:22, 23). God does not want a sacrifice if it is made in rebellion. He wants obedience. Rebellion and stubbornness are idolatry. They put self on the throne instead of God.

It was right for Bath-sheba to observe the ceremonial

laws of purification (Lev. 15:28), but that didn't make it all right for her to commit adultery with King David: "she came in unto him, and he lay with her; for she was purified from her uncleanness" (II Sam. 11:4).

It was right for the Pharisees to want to give gifts to God. It was wicked for them to use that as a dodge so they wouldn't have to care for their own parents (Mark 7:11).

It was right for the Jews to keep themselves undefiled for the eating of the Passover Lamb. But it was the height of hypocrisy for them to require the soldiers to break the legs of Jesus on the cross so He, the Passover Lamb Himself, would die before the sun went down, in order that they stay undefiled!

Can you see how people have taken lesser commands of God and used them as an excuse to break a major command?

I suppose that the area in which a woman most often wants to break the command of obedience to her husband is in her church attendance and offerings to the work of the Lord. It's right to go to church. It's right to give to God. Hebrews 10:25 says, "Not forsaking the assembling of ourselves together." It does not say it is a sin if a woman is not in church Sunday morning, Sunday night and Wednesday night prayer service!

Obviously there are situations when a woman cannot keep the command to assemble with Christians—her illness, the illness of a child, lack of transportation, being called out of town for an emergency. (Don't misunderstand: I know the surprising gamut of excuses people make for not attending church. They are excuses, not reasons. God holds them accountable for their care-lessness, you may be sure.) But God is not going to punish a woman who misses church when it was not possible for her to be there.

Neither will He punish a woman who misses church because her husband forbids her to go to church and she obeys him. (Certainly, if she misses church for any reason, she'll need to keep her spiritual life strong by careful attention to the Scripture and earnest prayer. Nor will she use that as an excuse for careless living. Still, God will hold her husband accountable if she can-not attend church because of his command.)

Again, if a woman feels a deep burden to give tithes and offerings to the Lord and her husband forbids it, the Scripture in Numbers 30 plainly says he has that right and that he will bear her iniquity. Isn't it wonderful that God sees the longings of a woman's heart? He rewards her, not for what she gives, but for what she yearns to give. "This poor widow hath cast more in, than all they which have cast into the treasury," Jesus said in Mark 12:43. Of the woman who gave two mites, Jesus said, "For all they did cast in of their abundance; but she of her want did cast in all that she had, even all her liv-ing" (vs. 44).

Don't forget that God owns the cattle on a thousand hills. We do not make Him poorer when we cannot give. We do enrich Him by our obedience.

Recently God answered prayer in a marvelous way for a friend I'll call Estelle. She felt led of God to pledge a certain amount for the church building fund. She asked her husband, and he said, "Certainly not. We can't possibly afford to give that much."

She asked me, "Since I earn the money, couldn't I use it for that if I felt led?"

(That was a hard question to ask a preacher's wife, when I knew how badly that money was needed!) But I sighed and shook my head.

"No, Estelle, do it God's way. Obey your husband, and let God take care of the needs of the church."

She cried some; for she loves the Lord, and she wants to serve Him. But she didn't mention it to her husband again.

A week later she came, just brimming with joy. "Guess what! I got a raise! It will total the exact amount I wanted to give to the Lord. And you know what? My husband says we can give it all!"

There are ways—there *are* ways God can bless the woman who follows her husband's leadership, ways she can still find joy in serving God!

Look at it this way: if you choose which commands you will obey and which you don't obey, you aren't obeying at all—you are doing all the time what you decided to do!

Would you let a child of yours obey that way? If your baby reached for the scissors, and you said, "No!" would you let the baby decide whether or not that was a reasonable command? "Don't be ridiculous," you'd say, "how could a baby know the danger in a pair of scissors?" Exactly!

Suppose you have a teenager who's been told never to use the car without permission. Suppose he does;

suppose he takes a group of young people from the church down to the rescue mission for a service. If, when you rebuked him, he said piously, "Well, Mom, I'm supposed to obey God, not man. God wanted me to serve Him this way," would you approve? Certainly not! No child could know all that was involved in using the car—and since when does the end justify wrong means? You don't let your children decide which orders they obey. Unless there is obedience all the time, there is no obedience any of the time. So, if you choose when to obey your husband, you are not obeying him at all. You are simply doing your own will, and sometimes it happens to coincide with his wishes.

So we'll agree that a woman may not obey a lesser command to thwart a major command of God.

What if a Husband Expressly Commands Something Explicitly Wrong?

But what if a husband expressly, positively, beyond the shadow of a doubt, commanded his wife to do something explicitly wrong, something plainly forbidden in Scripture? What if he told her to murder their child? What if he insisted she commit adultery? Do the Scriptures require her obedience under such circumstances?

When women ask me this question, I counter with two of my own:

1. "Have you been living in daily obedience to your husband as part of your wholehearted, loving submission to God?"

(This is an essential part of the problem. If a woman has not been submissive, God has no responsibility for her situation and cannot be blamed if her husband requires something wrong.)

2. "Has your husband ever actually commanded you to do something wrong?"

In the hundreds of times I have asked these questions, not once, if my memory is right, has a woman answered, "Yes, I am always obedient, and yet my husband has required me to break one of God's laws."

Never! Why?

Because, when a woman takes God at His Word, submits to her husband without reservation, fears God and loves Him, then God takes upon Himself the responsibility to see that a woman does not have to sin!

Don't misunderstand. I am aware that ungodly men sometimes demand things of their wives that are revolting and wrong. And you could perhaps add your own sad instances. But the fact remains that I have never known of a case where, when a woman said to her husband, "I will obey you implicitly, as if you were God, and trust you to make the right decisions for me," then set out to do it in loving, sweet, heart-yearning submission, he required her to do wrong.

Recently a girl whom I'll call Diane knocked on the door. "Libby," she wept, "I just found out that we are going to have a baby at last. But my husband says it upsets all his plans. He wants me to have an abortion. What shall I do?"

Now abortion is wrong, plainly wrong, beyond the shadow of a doubt. Should Diane do what her husband requires?

We prayed together, earnestly asking God to change her husband's heart about it. A week later she came again. "You wouldn't believe what has happened to my husband! He apologized, said he was wrong, says of course we'll have the baby, and love it, too!"

If God tells a woman to obey, then He performs whatever miracle is necessary to make her able to obey! It may be that we are no longer accustomed to expecting the intervention of an Almighty God in our personal lives. It may be that we don't expect miracles, and so God can't do any miracles. "He did not many mighty works there because of their unbelief" (Matt. 13:58). How blessed is the woman who will take God at His Word, believe Him, obey Him, and leave the consequences to Him!

God put a ram in the thicket so Abraham would not have to slay his son (Gen. 22:13). God arranged circumstances so David did not have to fight his own king (I Sam. 29:9–11). God made enough manna to fall on the sixth day so no one would have to break the Sabbath to get something to eat. God just does not make people choose between commands. He is not that kind of God!

I feel very deeply for a godly woman married to an unregenerate husband who seems to delight in torturing her and mocking her faith. I cannot say that the Scriptures guarantee a man will be saved if his wife wholeheartedly obeys him. I can assure you that there is no other way to win an unsaved husband except the way God has ordained—through a wife's loving, God-fearing obedience.

First Peter 3:1 says, "Likewise, ye wives, be in

subjection to your own husbands; that, if any obey not the word, they also may without the word be won by the conversation [behavior] of the wives." My husband tells me (he's the Greek scholar in this family) that "may be won" is in the simple future indicative tense, as if to say, "He will be saved."

First Corinthians 7:13 tells a woman who is married to an unsaved man, if he is pleased to dwell with her, not to leave him, "For what knowest thou, O wife, whether thou shalt save thy husband?" (vs. 16).

So the Scriptures indicate *the one way* to win an unsaved husband is to obey him cheerfully, from the heart, guarding the spiritual life.

A man always has the choice of saying yes or no to God. He can reject the pleadings of the Spirit, the pleas of his loving wife. If he does, and goes his own wicked way, then I have seen God reach down and take that man's life, rather than make a wife choose between two wrongs.

There is a striking example of this in the story of Nabal and Abigail, recorded in I Samuel 25. Nabal was a wicked, churlish man, evil in his doings, disagreeable, ungrateful to David for what he had done in protecting his livestock. David had asked him, in exchange, for food. Nabal, drunk and surly as usual, berated him; and David vowed to kill him and his family.

Abigail took upon herself Nabal's protection and quickly gave David what he asked. (There is no evidence she disobeyed Nabal. He was so drunk he didn't know what he was doing. And she reported to him what she had done as soon as he was sober enough to understand it.)

She did not berate her husband. But when she told him what she had done, he suffered a stroke of God; and in ten days he was dead. Did God, looking down, see Nabal's unyielding heart and take his life to spare Abigail any more heartache? Surely so. And so it will be, the Scripture seems to indicate, for any godly woman who obeys lovingly, from the heart, every command of God and her husband. If he will not change his ways and be worthy of such devotion, then God, it seems, will remove the obstruction.

God never gives two commands impossible to obey. He will never make a woman choose between two wrongs if she wholeheartedly follows the Scriptures.

Does God really mean it when He commands a wife to be in subjection to her husband? Without a doubt! It is a positive, direct command God expects to be obeyed, in faith, knowing and doing the will of God regardless of the consequences!

4

The Bible Examples

If God commands a woman to obey her husband without exception, and if He means it, then we should be able to find this in the experiences of Bible women. Did God honor obedience? Did He condemn disobedience?

We've already read in I Peter 3:5, "After this manner in the old time the holy women also, who trusted in God, adorned themselves, being in subjection unto their own husbands." In verse 6 Abraham's wife is singled out: "Even as Sara obeyed Abraham, calling him lord: whose daughters ye are, as long as ye do well, and are not afraid with any amazement."

Sarah's Relationship With Abraham

Sarah called Abraham "lord" even when talking to herself. She "laughed within herself, saying, After I am waxed old shall I have pleasure, my lord being old also?" (Gen. 18:12). She wasn't using the term sarcastically. She meant it.

After I led Arleen to the Lord, she asked me to pray with her about her husband's salvation. I showed her the Bible principle of submission, using I Peter, chapter 3. Later, she told me she went home and said to her husband, half-joking, half-complaining, "Okay, you're my lord and master, you big fat slob; what do you want me to do?"

As you've guessed, that isn't the meek and quiet spirit the Lord had in mind! (Arleen really did take to heart the lesson, and later her husband was saved.)

Sarah truly was an obedient wife. Abraham, in Egypt, fearing for his life because of his beautiful wife, asked her to lie for him, to say she was his sister, not his wife. (That was a half-truth; she was his half-sister.) She had a right to be uneasy and bitter about the whole affair, because Pharaoh took her into his household and might have taken her for his wife. But Sarah let God take care of it in His own good way. God did the needed miracle, a plague on the Pharaoh's house, to warn him. Sarah, in her obedience, was not subjected to the humiliation of being made a heathen king's concubine (Gen. 12:10–19).

But that sorry story didn't happen just once to Sarah. Later, in Genesis, chapter 20, the same thing happened with the king of Gerar. Again, God did a miracle in Sarah's behalf and spoke aloud to the heathen king to stop him from touching her (Gen. 20:1–18).

Sapphira and Ananias

There is a great difference in Sarah's obedience and the behavior of Sapphira, in Acts, chapter 5. Sapphira did not simply obey her husband when he decided to sell land and give a part to the Lord, claiming to give it all.

She actively conspired with him to tempt the Holy Spirit. They "agreed together" to lie (Acts 5:9). God killed Sapphira, not because she obeyed her husband but because she wanted to do wrong, wanted the praise of man, and conspired with her husband to get it. The word *privy,* in verse 2, as translated in the KJV, means "hidden or clandestine, furtive, secretly cognizant, privately aware as a party to the act." Sapphira did not lie because her husband commanded her to. She conspired with Ananias, and God held her accountable for it.

David's Wife Michal

Michal, daughter of King Saul, David's first, passionate love, is an example of God's punishment on a rebellious wife. David was still only a shepherd boy (though anointed king) when word came that Saul would be pleased for him to ask for Michal. He risked death by killing two hundred Philistines for her dowry, and she gladly went to be his wife. She saved his life and risked her father's paranoid anger when Saul tried to kill him. After David fled to the wilderness, Saul betrothed Michal to another man. Ten long years passed before David could reclaim his wife.

After the kingdom was established, David brought back the ark of God which had been at the house of Obed-edom for twenty long, sad years. It was an exhilarating day when David brought back the ark to Jerusalem— the manifest presence of God Himself with His people! David could not contain his delight: he "danced before the Lord with all his might." Michal watched from the window and despised him. (Why? We can only guess. But many a woman has been jealous of her husband's love for God.)

When David came to his own home to bless his own family, fulfilling his high-priestly obligation to his own, Michal reviled him. The sin of her rebellion was compounded because she hated him for his goodness, for his joy in the Lord, not for wickedness.

The result? "Therefore Michal the daughter of Saul had no child unto the day of her death" (II Sam. 6:23). But God's punishment was not ended. She adopted the five sons of her sister. All five of them were slain to atone for King Saul's breaking an oath made to the Gibeonites (II Sam. 21:8, 9). God does not lightly regard a woman's rebellion against her husband.

Is there any instance in the Bible where a woman disobeyed her husband and she was commended for it? Many Bible scholars say, "Yes, in the disobedience of Queen Vashti toward King Ahasuerus." I do not know that we need to justify the actions of a pagan queen in a pagan court; but since the theory is so widespread (and since fools rush in where angels fear to tread!), let's look at the Scripture and see if God did approve of Vashti's disobedience. You'll find the story in Esther, chapters 1 and 2.

Queen Vashti and Queen Esther

The reasons some Bible teachers commend Vashti's disobedience are these:

1. King Ahasuerus ("Xerxes") commanded Vashti to do something sinful. It was the custom in those days for women to be veiled in the presence of men.

2. The name of God is not found in the book of Esther. It is a book of men's acts, not God's.

3. If Mordecai and Esther had been godly, they would have been back in the land of Judah with the spiritually minded returnees after the captivity.

Therefore, they say, it was right for Vashti to disobey her husband. A careful reading of the entire book of Esther will not support this, it seems to me.

King Ahasuerus was a wicked man: secular history confirms it. But nothing is told in this Scripture about Ahasuerus that reveals him so. Ahasuerus gave a feast but permitted great freedom to his guests. He did not force any man to drink wine. "The drinking was according to the law; none did compel" (Esther 1:8). The kings of Persia had learned from godly Jews like Daniel that they would not defile themselves with wine (Dan. 1:8). This king was an absolute monarch, but he did not here behave like a tyrant.

What did Ahasuerus ask his wife to do? The Bible says he commanded her to come before the king "with the crown royal, to shew the people and the princes her beauty: for she was fair to look on" (1:11). Did he ask her to commit a sin? There is no indication that he did. It was not against any command of God for her to "show her beauty." Josephus, the Jewish historian, said Ahasuerus asked her to come naked. The Bible does not say so and does not imply it. Would it have been a sin for her to come unveiled, even if it were the custom? No, for "custom" is not necessarily God's law. "Howbeit in vain do they worship me," Jesus said, "teaching for doctrines the commandments of men" (Mark 7:7).

An interesting passage in Herodotus (Book V, 18) says King Darius (the father of this King Ahasuerus) told the Macedonians, "We Persians have a custom when we make a great feast to bring with us to the board our wives and concubines, and make them sit beside us." So Ahasuerus may not have required anything at all out of the ordinary when he sent for Vashti, and there is certainly no evidence that he commanded her to sin.

When she refused to come, Ahasuerus reacted with remarkable restraint. The man who reigned from India to Ethiopia, over 127 provinces, was obviously accustomed to being obeyed. You'd expect him to order Vashti's immediate death. Instead, he reasonably sought advice of his wise men "for so was the king's manner" (1:13). His punishment was mild, considering her crime. And the emphasis in the letters sent to the provinces stresses not the insult to the king but the need for every man to bear rule in his own house (1:20, 22).

Ahasuerus' pride in Vashti's beauty was evidently not wrong, since the Bible stresses the great beauty of Esther as well.

In contrast, the characteristic of Esther most stressed is that she was obedient to Mordecai (2:10, 20; 4:15, 16). Why is it stressed? On purpose, perhaps, to contrast it with Vashti's disobedience.

It was no mark of unspirituality for a Jew to be in Shushan at this time. God had told the people to settle down in captivity, to build houses, plant gardens, and bear children there (Jer. 29:5, 7). Daniel never returned to Jerusalem. Nehemiah went back and forth but did not stay (Neh. 2:6; 5:14; 13:6).

Nor were all the people who went back to Jerusalem spiritually minded. That was the whole burden of the preaching of the prophets Haggai and Zechariah.

Actually, Mordecai was a spiritually minded man. He risked death by not bowing down to Haman, because he would honor God above all others.

Esther was a sweet Christian girl. Her influence was strong enough to win the hearts of her servant girls, so she could promise they would pray with her. It was strong enough to touch the heart of the king himself. She was brave, too. She was not content to save just the lives of her own household (Esther 8:6). She achieved that; then she risked her life to make sure the thousands of Jews scattered throughout the empire were also saved.

When the Jews in Shushan got permission to fight for their lives, they exercised great restraint. They never "took of the prey"—they did not enrich themselves by the goods of those who had plotted their deaths.

Is the blessing of God portrayed in the book, even if His name is not there? Certainly! His careful guidance and protection are shown in every chapter.

It seems safe to conclude that Esther was blessed of God because she was obedient, and that Vashti lost her favored position because she refused to obey her husband. You may not agree; but at least you will concede, won't you, that the story ought not to be used to try to approve a woman's disobedience to her husband?

The overwhelming weight of Bible testimony about a wife's obedience is that God expects a woman to obey her husband cheerfully, immediately and without reservation.

5

Don't I Have Any Rights?

"It just doesn't seem fair," you wail. "Can't I ever do what I want to do? Don't I have any rights at all?" You picture yourself as a Victorian housewife, long-skirted and fully bustled, bending over a scrub bucket and string mop, pushing back a tendril of hair from your sweating face. You picture your husband, mustached and glowering, standing over you with a whip. "If I do what you are saying," you argue, "I'll just be a plain old slave. Don't I have any rights?"

Can you find a Kleenex somewhere and mop up the tears, just for a minute, long enough to talk to me about what your rights really are?

For you—and I—don't have any rights, no rights at all. We lost them on the day we rebelled against God. We lost them, not because we are women, but because we are sinners.

Romans 3:23 says all have sinned. That must include you. Romans 6:23 says that the wages of sin is death or Hell. If you got your rights, if you got what you truly deserve, you would go to Hell. If, by the mercy of God, you have accepted His gift of eternal life, then you have been forgiven for your sin, and the penalty has been paid. (Romans 6:23 concludes: "But the gift of God is eternal life through Jesus Christ our Lord.")

Now, if Jesus paid the penalty of your sin for you, you don't belong to yourself anymore; you belong to Him. The rights you once possessed now are His, the One who bought your salvation and freedom from death.

The price He paid for your salvation was not cheap. "Ye were not redeemed with corruptible things, as silver and gold, from your vain conversation received by tradition from your fathers; But with the precious blood of Christ" (I Pet. 1:18, 19).

That's why the Apostle Paul asked, "What? know ye not that your body is the temple of the Holy Ghost which is in you, which ye have of God, and ye are not your own? For ye are bought with a price: therefore glorify God in your body, and in your spirit, which are God's" (I Cor. 6:19, 20). We just don't belong to ourselves anymore. Jesus bought us and owns us, heart and body.

Slaves really don't have any rights. That's the meaning of Romans 6:18: "Being then made free from sin, ye became the servants [or bondslaves] of righteousness."

We are slaves to Christ. But don't forget we had already lost our rights. It was our poverty and bondage to sin that drove us to Him.

If we are servants, we ought to be glad to do anything He tells us to do. Jesus illustrated this when He took off His outer garments, girded Himself with a towel, and washed the feet of the disciples. "I have given you an example," He explained in John 13:15–17, "that ye should do as I have done to you. Verily, verily, I say unto you, The servant is not greater than his lord; neither he that is sent greater than he that sent him. If ye know these things, happy are ye if ye do them."

In fact, that is the background of the passage in I Peter 3 which we've already read together: "*Likewise, ye wives, be in subjection to your own husbands.*"

We are to be in subjection "likewise." Likewise to what? You'll find the answer in the preceding chapter (I Pet. 2:21-23): "For even hereunto were ye called: because Christ also suffered for us, leaving us an example, that ye should follow his steps: Who did no sin, neither was guile found in his mouth: Who, when he was reviled, reviled not again; when he suffered, he threatened not; but committed himself to him that judgeth righteously.... Likewise, ye wives, be in subjection." Like whom? Like Jesus! The submission of the Lord Jesus is our example. He submitted not just to the tender ministrations of the Father. He submitted to revilings and curses, persecution and suffering. He was our example, not just to obey a gentle and kind husband but a harsh and mean husband as well.

You may find that your obedience to your husband and your obedience to God are all tied together. You may not want to obey your husband because you are living in rebellion against God. I would be especially dubious about my spiritual dedication if I found myself using a "spiritual" reason as an excuse not to obey my husband. Rebellion in the one area is caused by rebellion in the other.

We've said you have no rights—but that's only half

the story. The Christian wife has no rights; she's a bondslave—but how wonderful are the privileges that come with being a bondslave of Christ!

Privilege means "a special law made to a single individual." You have no rights under the law; but God has made special laws, privileges, for His children. What are they? That He makes us not bondslaves but His children. "For ye have not received the spirit of bondage again to fear; but ye have received the Spirit of adoption, whereby we cry, Abba, Father. The Spirit itself beareth witness with our spirit, that we are the children of God: And if children, then heirs; heirs of God, and joint-heirs with Christ" (Rom. 8:15–17). The crowning glory is found in verse 32: "He that spared not his own Son, but delivered him up for us all, how shall he not with him also freely give us all things?"

You have no natural rights—you sold them for cheap, sensual satisfaction—but you have the privileges that come with receiving Christ as your Saviour! You need no longer to be a slave to sin but a slave to Christ—no, not a slave, because He adopts you into the family of God and makes you an heir alongside your big Brother, Jesus. Everything He will inherit from the Father is also yours. When the Father gave us Jesus, He gave us everything.

What are the promises in the Scripture given to every Christian—promises of joy, satisfaction of need, peace, forgiveness of sin, promises that someday we will see His dear face and be like Him? Those promises are yours. They belong to you as surely as to any soul redeemed by Christ. Have you claimed your privileges?

Or have you been so busy defending your non-existent rights you haven't taken time to delight in all you do possess?

You Can Expect God to Keep His Promises

Specifically, you have the privilege of expecting God to keep His promises. Psalm 37:3–5 says, "Trust in the Lord, and do good; so shalt thou dwell in the land, and verily thou shalt be fed. Delight thyself also in the Lord; and he shall give thee the desires of thine heart. Commit thy way unto the Lord; trust also in him; and he shall bring it to pass." This plainly promises that, if you obey the Scriptures and concern yourself with the Lord's will and His plans, you can have the desires of your heart. The requirement? Simple faith and a commitment to do the whole will of God. The result? The desires of your heart!

We have said before that the life of submission to your husband is a life of faith, faith that the God who requires you to obey will make it possible for you to obey. Certainly faith is involved, faith in the God of Heaven and earth who is able to do anything we ask (or even think, Ephesians 3:20 says). Not only is He able to do it for us, He wants to do it, yearns to help us, grieves when our lack of faith thwarts His giving to us!

You Can Choose Which Man You Will Obey

Second, a woman has the privilege of choosing which man she will obey. She needs to obey only her own husband, not every man!

"Wives, submit yourselves unto your own husbands."—Eph. 5:22.

"Wives, submit yourselves unto your own husbands."—Col. 3:18.

"Obedient to their own husbands."—Titus 2:5.

"Wives, be in subjection to your own husbands."—I Pet. 3:1.

Have you ever realized how fortunate you are that you choose the man you marry and obey? You didn't get to choose your parents and had to obey them anyway. You couldn't choose the teachers you had to obey. You have little choice, practically speaking, about the civil authorities you obey. But the one single authority most pervasive and direct in your life—that authority you may choose!

It's true that loving a man isn't enough to make obeying him easy. It takes more than love to obey a man day after day and year after year. It takes character! Still, it's a marvelous provision of God that He lets a woman fall deeply in love with the man she is to obey.

Does a wife have the right to expect her husband to make her happy? We have the feeling she does, perhaps because when we were girls, we read so many romances with so-they-fell-in-love-and-got-married-and-lived-happily-ever-after endings. But the truth is, there is no man on earth who can make you happy. He can provide for your welfare and supply your physical needs, but he cannot guarantee your happiness. His total love and devotion will not make you happy. Even if a man tried to satisfy your every expectation, you'd be frustrated by his adaptability!

No, no man can make you happy. It is Jesus only, Himself alone, who will meet your deepest yearnings and longings. You must find your satisfaction in the Lord if you are going to be happy. You do not have a right to expect your husband to make you happy.

(I hasten to add that I believe the marriage of a godly man and woman, based on Bible principles, brings mutual delight and blessing unmatched by any other earthly relationship.)

You Receive a Husband's Lifelong Concern for Your Welfare

Not only do you have the privilege of a heavenly inheritance, and not only do you have the privilege of choosing the man you marry and obey; you also have the privilege of a husband's lifelong loving devotion and concern for your welfare.

The same passage in Ephesians, chapter 5, which tells a woman she must obey her husband in everything also has clear, unbelievable instructions for her husband. "Husbands, love your wives," Ephesians 5:25 instructs, *"even as Christ also loved the church, and gave himself for it"*!

God expects a man to love his wife with such passion, such devotion, such commitment, that he would gladly die for her! A wife must give her complete obedience to her husband, just as a good Christian obeys Jesus. On her husband's part, God expects him to act with the same unselfish, eternal care that Christ gives to us Christians!

Can you imagine the awesome task a man takes upon himself when he assumes the lifetime responsibility of a wife and family? Food, clothing, shelter, the automobile, training of the children—all these a godly man commits himself to for the rest of his life!

No matter how he feels, he must go out into the world each day to earn the money to feed the family and pay the bills. No matter if the company he works for lays off workers, including him; no matter if his job is replaced by a machine; no matter if he has a case of the "blahs" or a toothache or the flu—God says it is his responsibility to put food on the table and a roof over the head of his family that day.

An old rhyme says, "Man works from sun to sun, but a woman's work is never done." And it's true that a woman's work is never done. How do I know? Because we have seven children, that's how I know! But it's also true for a man.

A wife ought to understand how much a man gives her when he gives her his name and his pledge to care for her until they are parted by death.

You Have Freedom From the Burden of Decision-Making

You have another privilege. (You thought it was a liability, but you'll discover it's a privilege!) You have freedom from having to take the consequences of making decisions. When you give back to your husband the responsibility for the direction of the home and the making of decisions, you also give him the responsibility for the consequences of his decisions. My friend Marty said it this way: "When I found out Dave was supposed to be the head of this family, it sure made life simple. Now he makes the decisions, and he's stuck with them!"

Fortunately, that's the way a man likes it. God made a man to be aggressive, to respond to challenge, to glory in his manhood, to rejoice in draining his strength, to risk great hazards for the one he loves. It is his very aggressiveness that a woman sometimes finds frightening, simply because she is a woman. She may not have confidence in her physical strength, in her ability to cope with danger, in her decision-making ability. It is a privilege for a woman to have a man take upon himself her welfare.

Many of the disagreements that come up in a marriage stem from this basic difference of man and woman. If I had my "druthers," the Handford family might never buy a car or a home! Those big numbers written out on a solemn sales contract frighten me. Yet to my husband, the responsibility of buying a car or a home or whatever else is needed, is part of his commitment to this family. He can, and will, pay for it. Of course we talk over important purchases; he would not commit us to a course of action I had major reservations about. Nevertheless, he holds himself responsible for meeting our bills.

"But when my husband spends too much money on other things," you protest, "I'm the one who has to pinch pennies. It always has to come out of the grocery money, and that doesn't seem fair."

You're right about where the pinch comes. Food purchases are a major living expense in most households and one of the few unfixed costs. Often the only place you can squeeze out money is in buying cheaper groceries. In that sense, beyond a doubt, a wife pays the consequences of her husband's financial decisions.

But she'll pay consequences far more serious if she usurps his right to make those decisions. If she manages the money to "keep that poor idiot from driving us to the poorhouse," she had better get used to the task of worrying all the time about where the money is coming from. No man, stripped of his pride in providing for his family, will show much concern about the bills. How much better it is to let him make the decisions and let him cope with the consequences and, when needed, pinch the pennies in grocery buying! God has a wonderful way of working it out for the comfort of the whole family when a woman commits herself to her husband's leadership.

This may seem especially hard to a woman who is working outside the home, earning perhaps as much money as her husband. If they each think of the money they earn as "mine," finances will become a source of real conflict. In my judgment, if only the husband is earning money, the money he brings home is "theirs," not "his," because the wife contributes energy, thought, labor to the home just as surely as the husband working outside the home. In the same way, perhaps, when both husband and wife are working outside the home, they need to think of their income not as "his" or "hers" but "theirs" and apply the same biblical principles in their finances as in every other aspect of their lives together.

Two Really Are Better Than One

But the greatest privilege a loving, submissive wife has is that of being a helpmeet to her husband. King Solomon said it simply: "Two are better than one; because they have a good reward for their labour. For if they fall, the one will lift up his fellow: but woe to him that is alone when he falleth; for he hath not another to help him up. Again, if two lie together, then they have heat: but how can one be warm alone? And if one prevail against him, two shall withstand him; and a threefold cord is not quickly broken" (Eccl. 4:9–12).

There is a wonder, a multiplication in the union of a man and woman, far more than either of them could accomplish alone. It isn't the simple addition of $1 + 1 = 2$. It is a miraculous multiplying of strength such as God promised the Israelites when five could chase an hundred, but an hundred would put ten thousand of the enemy to flight (Lev. 26:8).

A good woman, deeply loving her husband, happily submissive, earnestly praying for him, eager to help him—a good woman can inspire a man to service far beyond what he could have dreamed of alone.

But it's all tied together with a woman's obeying her husband, perhaps because her honest dependence draws forth his exultant effort.

Rollo May, in his book, *Love and Will,* tells of a Greek island where no woman has set foot in five hundred years. The monks who live there, he says, are effeminate in voice and action. Why? A man needs a truly womanly woman to stir his instinctive manliness.

This marriage is not a 50-50 proposition. (People who must measure their "50%" never can agree where the line is anyway.) This marriage is 100% and 100%; total, wholehearted commitment, all the way. She does everything she can think of to make him happy. She does everything she is humanly capable of doing for his sake. Then she trusts God to work in her husband's heart whatever is needed there.

Notice what alchemy her love and devotion provide. Proverbs 31:10-12 says, "Who can find a virtuous woman? for her price is far above rubies. The heart of her husband doth safely trust in her, so that he shall have no need of spoil. She will do him good and not evil all the days of her life."

This good woman, this obedient woman, has earned the complete trust of her husband. Since she is committed to doing what he wants her to do, there is no conflict of interest. He knows she won't betray him before business associates or friends. Her every act, her every thought, does him good.

Verse 23 says her husband is "known in the gates" and that he "sitteth among the elders of the land." Her husband has risen to great honor; he is a leader in the city. That is listed as a fruit of the virtuous woman. Why? Because a virtuous woman supports her husband, encourages him, makes it possible for him to be a leader of men. Verse 28 says her children will call her blessed and her husband will praise her.

Is this obedient woman a wimp, a doormat, a mindless robot doing only whatever it is her husband capriciously decides? Oh, I hope you will not get that impression!

When God said, "It is not good that the man should be alone; I will make him an help meet for him" (Gen. 2:18), He made it abundantly evident that a man has lacks, weaknesses, insufficiencies. If a wife does not bring into her marriage every skill, every gift and talent, every womanly perception—her total heart and mind and moral conviction—then she in effect robs her husband of what he woefully needs!

This godly, faithful, obedient woman will be used of God to enrich the whole world!

There have been great men of God who served God well without the help of a good wife. I'll never forget the pathos in the voice of an evangelist who said privately, "My wife is a good woman, and I love her, but she isn't spiritually minded. She doesn't share my burden for souls. There will always be some areas we cannot share."

I have often wondered if Job's wife ever regretted not being a helpmeet to him in his terrible testing. He sat on an ash heap; his body, a revulsive mass of boils; children, house, land destroyed. He needed someone, only one, to care, to comfort him. There was one who could have helped. She had lived with him, borne his children, knew better than anyone else on earth the uprightness of Job's life. But when he begged her to help him, she ignored him. "My breath is strange to my wife, though I entreated for the children's sake of mine own body" (Job 19:17). What regret Job's wife must have felt when God "turned his captivity," vindicated his righteousness, and gave him double for all he suffered! Her failure must have haunted her the rest of her life!

As I say, there have been great men of God used in spite of the women they married. But how many men have been encouraged and strengthened by the hands of a good woman and inspired to do great service for the Lord far beyond what they could have done alone! When a man says, upon receiving an honor, "I could not have done it without the help of my wife," you can believe it is nearly always the honest truth.

A good woman who marries a good man can multiply his service to God a thousandfold. And that's a privilege beyond all speaking!

~~ 6 ~~

But What About the Problems?

"All right," you may say wearily, "you've convinced me. I agree that the Bible says I ought to obey my husband. I agree God meant what He says. I agree that I can help my husband by being obedient. But when you get down to the nitty-gritty business of living it, there sure are a heap of problems."

Don't I Ever Get to Express an Opinion?

Certainly you get to express an opinion. If you are a submissive, loving wife, your husband will want your input, your wisdom. Because he asked for it, he will value it more highly and consider it more objectively. Opinions constantly expressed, when unsought, have a tendency to sound like criticism; and most of us don't enjoy criticism.

When you are talking over a problem, if it isn't asking too much, try to think reasonably. (That sentence sounds like a man wrote it. Sorry about that!) Men think women talk too much about how they feel rather than considering facts. Sure, it's important how you feel.

Can you tell him why you feel that way?

For the same reason, try not to bring unrelated problems into the discussion. Sometimes I hear myself saying, "But, honey, you always do that—remember back when you . . . ?" and I know I've lost it. Try to keep your discussion to the problem at hand and not bring in unrelated events from the past.

And, if you can possibly avoid it (I have to use Scotch tape over my mouth), don't say, "I told you so." If events prove you right (and they may), you can be sure he knows it. If he took a wrong road when you meekly suggested the other one, don't you know that every turn of the wheel on the way back says its own "I told you so"? If you keep pushing for an apology, he may remember some times when you were wrong; and you'll lose all your points in that game.

Actually, in a wholesome, working, husband-wife relationship, there will be a free flow of ideas and suggestions, some give-and-take and some good-natured banter. A wife can express her reasons openly, frankly, and resort to tears only when really necessary. (By that, I don't mean you ought to try to manipulate him with tears. I mean you ought to let him know when it is a matter you care very deeply about.)

In this wholesome, working relationship, the husband, in his turn, can express his thinking, his reservations, his feelings. They together will discuss the pros and cons cheerfully, try to make the decision not on who deserves to win the argument but rather "What is best for this family?" She can remind him of anything she feels would help him in making the decision. But both of them know that the final decision is his and that God holds him accountable for it.

You've heard, surely, about the husband and wife who went fishing. He said, "Hand me those shears."

She said, "You mean, 'Hand me those scissors.'"

"Give me those shears."

"Scissors?"

"Shears!"

Exasperated, he shoved her overboard. As she sank from sight, she held up two fingers, cutting the air. Scissors!

That has become my private signal to my husband. It says, "Okay, honey, I give up. You're the boss. Guess I can't win them all!"

Please learn from that quaint tale, not to die rather than change your mind, but to accept his decisions gracefully!

A sweet example of a wife's quiet contribution to a family problem is found in the relationship of Manoah and his wife, the parents of Samson. An angel announced to the wife that she would have a child. She told Manoah about it, and he told her to let him know when the angel came again. But when the angel did come, Manoah said, "We shall surely die, because we have seen God."

Her serene response was, 'If the Lord were going to kill us, He wouldn't have taken our offerings and wouldn't have told us about the baby' (Judges 13:23).

With such quiet reminders, a wife can be a helpmeet to her husband.

But My Husband Won't Take the Leadership of Our Home

Women often complain that the husband will not assume his responsibility as head of the home. He seems to be content to let his wife run things. When God speaks to her heart about submitting to his authority, and she tries to, sometimes it seems he doesn't want to take charge. What can a wife do then?

It's important to remember you are not merely *permitting* him to be boss. You aren't giving him the privilege, not saying, "All right, you can drive for awhile until I want to." If it is done that way, then you are not letting him rule, whatever words you use. Perhaps the husband senses that and is unwilling to undergo the upheaval that kind of decision creates. Your attitude has to be: "I am taking my proper place. I am going to obey you in everything."

It's likely, if you have been making the decisions for the family, that you aren't even aware that you do it. You may feel like your husband has full say, that you defer to his judgment. Take a good, critical look at yourself. When you are invited out to dinner, who makes the decision? When the children come to request permission to go somewhere, which parent do they ask? These are pretty good indications of who is running the home.

Most men hate "scenes." They despise confusion and disorder. They will go to almost any length to have peace in their homes. They will let a woman have her way rather than argue and quarrel. But the price a man has to pay is the price of his manhood. Before you complain that your husband won't take the leadership of your home, search your heart carefully. Do you really rely on his judgment? Are you willing to commit yourself to his decisions? If not, don't complain that he will not lead. For the sake of peace, he may not fight for his authority. Your habit of bossing may be more deeply ingrained than you possibly realize.

Don't mistake a man's gentleness for weakness. Don't mistake a quietly spoken word for vacillation. A gentle man can still lead his home as competently, if not as flamboyantly, as an aggressive man. And a loving wife who leans on her husband will call forth his strength and manliness.

How can you give the leadership back to him? Admit your failure. Ask his forgiveness. Then simply give him the opportunity to make the decisions. Send the children to him for permissions. Let him decide when you do what. (You realize this won't work, don't you, if he makes a decision and you say, "What in the world did you do that for?") If you stop bossing the family, he will be the boss automatically.

A friend I'll call Edna learned this to her genuine surprise and pleasure. She's a strong, big woman, smart, competent, mother of four husky teenage boys. Her husband is quiet, soft-spoken. When she first heard she was supposed to obey her husband, she snorted, "It won't work!" But the Holy Spirit convicted her, so she said, "All right, I'll try." When the boys would come to her for permission, she would sweetly say, "Ask your father." When a decision needed to be made about painting the house or buying a new appliance or the thousand and one important decisions that have to be made for a family, she kept her mouth closed. Imagine her delight when her husband assumed an interest in the home he had never had before and guided the family with a sureness she had never seen before. "It works! I've never been so happy in my life," she said.

Gayle said to me, "I want Joe to take charge of this family, and he won't. He makes me make the hard decisions and do the discipline. I told him he needed to make our son Tim straighten up and do right, and he said he thought I was being too hard on him. I wish my husband *would* take charge!"

Gayle had fallen into the trap of thinking she wanted her husband to lead, not realizing that, when he did lead, but in a direction she didn't think he ought to go, she didn't want to follow him.

A common area of problem is in family devotions. A family ought every day to meet around the Word of God and pray for mutual needs. If the father will not take the leadership about family devotions, should the mother?

A woman could ask her husband what time of day he prefers the family have devotions. Then she could arrange meals, bedtimes, or whatever was needed, so the family was organized and ready at the time he set for Bible reading. She can make it as easy as possible for him to say, "Time for devotions."

If he requires her to lead the family devotions, then she can do it in meekness, always leaving the family circle open for him to come in.

What if My Husband Won't Actually Forbid Me to Do Something but Says He'd Rather I Didn't?

Remember we are talking about a heart attitude of submission, not a letter-of-the-law obedience. So you ought not to disobey your husband just because he forgot to say the magic words, "I forbid it." You won't be looking for loopholes; you will be sincerely trying to please him.

At the same time, if he is unsaved or an untaught Christian, he may not be spiritually minded. "For they that are after the flesh do mind the things of the flesh; but they that are after the Spirit the things of the Spirit" (Rom. 8:5). You shouldn't be surprised if there are some parts of your life you and your unsaved husband don't feel the same about. "Can two walk together, except they be agreed?" (Amos 3:3). It is almost inevitable that an unspiritual husband would not understand your hunger for spiritual things. He may not be willing to forbid you but still find your spiritual needs incomprehensible. If he gives you ungrudging permission, then certainly it is right to do it.

Even then, it seems to me, a husband ought to feel very sure he has first place in your heart. Can a husband be jealous of a wife's love for the church and her pastor? Certainly! Too often a wife quotes the preacher or the church as the authority in her life. No wonder he feels "low man on the totem pole" and jealous of his wife's love of spiritual things.

You can find many ways to make your husband feel he is the most important human being in your life. (And it's right for him to feel that. God does not suffer when you love your husband with your whole heart. Loving the Lord wholeheartedly should help you to love your husband more.) You ought to enjoy and share your husband's interests. Not all of them are wrong—some things he likes you can share with real enthusiasm. If you show keen and genuine interest in his affairs, he'll less likely be jealous of your spiritual activities.

Nor will you want to use your husband's diffidence about spiritual things as an excuse for not doing right. If he permits you to go to church on Sunday morning, even if he doesn't prefer it, then why not get Sunday dinner in the oven before you go to church so his Sunday schedule is not disrupted? If he suggests you go dancing with him and you explain that you are uncomfortable with the idea of dancing with other men and he understands and yields to your feelings, then you need not go dancing. The whole import of the Scriptures in I Peter 3 is that a woman who obeys her husband will also earnestly work at being a good Christian all the time.

What if His Commands Are Contradictory?

They may be. Husbands, like wives, are human and sometimes don't know what they want! Sometimes a man will say something in anger, not meaning it at all, and both you and he know he didn't mean it.

In the midst of an argument, one husband said to his wife, "Why don't you just get out of the house?" So she did! Later she told me, very sanctimoniously, "He

told me to leave, and since I'm an obedient wife, I left!''
Actually, she was a rebellious wife, and her rebellion
nearly destroyed the home.

Jackie had a different problem. "My husband
drinks," she said. "He'll lose his driver's license if the
police catch him driving when he's drunk one more time.
But if he's drinking, he insists I give him the car keys.
I've been trying to obey him, like you told me to. Is it
right for me to give him the car keys and endanger people's lives like that?"

"Have you ever asked him when he is sober what
he wants you to do about it?"

"Oh, yes. Then he tells me I must be sure *not* to give
him the keys when he's drinking."

"I think that is your answer. You are doing what
he basically wants you to do. Perhaps, when he's been
drinking, you could offer to drive him where he needs
to go."

That's what Jackie did. And after two years of
earnest prayer, her husband was saved.

Another friend has a husband who is an earnest,
good Christian, but he is a "brittle" diabetic. His blood
sugar is extremely hard to stabilize, and he often hovers
between insulin coma and sugar shock. When it gets out
of balance, he is extremely irritable and unreasonable.
His wife has learned this; so when he starts demanding
something totally unlike himself, she knows they must
get to the doctor at once. This same sort of compassionate
understanding of a man's frailties is needed in the case
of mental illness.

How Can I Be a Good Christian if He Won't Let Me Go to Church?

Let's ask that question another way: "How can you be a good Christian if you don't obey the plain command of God to obey your husband?" The first step of Christian growth is surrender of our own will to God's will. The most important way to be a good Christian is to obey God's commands.

Admittedly it is hard to be a good Christian without fellowship with other Christians, without good Bible preaching. But you do have the Word of God. You have the Holy Spirit, the best Teacher you could possibly have, who "will guide you into all truth" (John 16:13). You can be a strong Christian nurtured only by the Word of God, taught only by the Holy Spirit. It is not easy to be a good Christian without Christian fellowship, but you can do it and be the stronger for having had to stand alone for awhile. Think, too, of what joy and fellowship you will have someday with the husband won by your submission, as you serve the Lord together!

Why Do I Have to Make All the Concessions?

Why doesn't the husband have to do his part first? Why? Because you are the one burdened for a Christian home. Having a home where Christ is the head is cheap enough at whatever price you have to pay! Think how long the rewards of a good Christian home will last. Then ask yourself if it is worth the trifling mortifications of obedience. Of course it is! All valuable things cost something. Certainly you will have to pay a price.

A girl I'll call Sue phoned. Her voice sounded panicky. "Libby, come quick. Everything's fallen apart!"

I hurried to their home, dreading some catastrophic news. Sue and her husband had just weathered a stormy time of adjustment, and I could hardly imagine what could have gone wrong now.

"Just look," she cried, pointing to two ordinary-looking, beat-up shoes lying inside the front door.

"Yes?"

"Tom leaves stuff where he drops it all the time. All day long I have to pick up after that man. This is the last straw! You can't even walk in the door without falling over his things!"

I giggled. (A pastor's wife shouldn't, I know—after all, how many times am I equally as foolish?) "Sue, if you picked up every sock, every dirty shirt, every sticky pair of pants Tom leaves down, all day long, how much time would it take?"

She wrinkled her forehead. Then it was her turn to giggle. "Maybe twenty minutes."

"Is it worth your spending twenty minutes a day to have a happy home?"

She threw up her hands in surrender. "Okay, I get it. No more preaching. Yeah, I'll pick up his old dirty clothes and love him anyway." And she did! Six years and four children later she's still picking up after Tom and enjoying her happy home.

There is another merit in obedience even when you feel you are making all the concessions. Heartfelt obedience will reveal to you your own deficiencies, your own failures. It will awaken in you a sense of need for the cleansing of the Holy Spirit in your own life.

Peggy said one day, "My husband isn't spiritually minded at all. I wish he were like the pastor. I want him to be a good example to the kids, to earn the respect of our teenagers. Oh, he's a good man, but he hasn't been saved very long, and he just doesn't show all the fruits of the Spirit he ought to show."

I asked her gently (it's easy to hurt when you are trying to help), "But Peggy, are you demanding more of him than you demand of yourself? Are you really doing all that you ought to do about your own spiritual life? Wouldn't it be better to ask God to show you your failures and let Him deal with your husband as He sees best?"

She looked surprised, then angry, then ashamed. She answered slowly, "I see what you mean. I've been thinking I was the good one, that I was making all the sacrifices—when actually I've been very critical. Yes, you're right; I am the one who needs to make some changes."

But I Love the Lord, and I Want to Serve Him

Good! Then do what He commanded. Servants don't choose what they are to do. They do what they are told (Luke 17:10). The best service you can ever do for God is to have a Christian home. So obey your husband. Let that home be a source of blessing to the whole world.

It may be your husband will let you do some Christian service in your home. You could have Child Evangelism classes or a Five-Day Club. You could win that lonely neighbor to the Lord over a cup of coffee. You could choose a rowdy neighborhood kid to be your special project, lead him to Christ, and help him get established in his Christian life. There are many ways to serve the Lord without leaving your home.

It's true that most of a woman's service to God will be plain, hard, physical work. (That's probably true for a man as well.) If you read Proverbs 31 and Isaiah 58 concerning a woman's ministries, you'll get the strong impression that the Christian woman works very hard, doing things with her hands, to serve the Lord.

Even if your husband will not permit any outward Christian service, you still serve God when you love Him and praise Him. "By him therefore let us offer the sacrifice of praise to God continually, that is, the fruit of our lips giving thanks" (Heb. 13:15).

But I Made a Mistake When I Married Him

The Bible plainly forbids marriage between a believer and unbeliever—an "unequal yoke" (II Cor. 6:14). But just as plainly it teaches that, when a man and woman are united in marriage, even if one is unsaved, the marriage is not to be broken. "What therefore God hath joined together," Matthew 19:6 says, "let not man put asunder." God joined the two together. God Himself performs the miracle of making of one flesh a man and woman. Because He joined them, they are joined for life. "The woman which hath an husband that believeth not, and if he be pleased to dwell with her, let her not leave him" (I Cor. 7:13). It may be you were young and ignorant and did not know the teaching of Scripture concerning marriage with an unbeliever. Perhaps you came to the Lord after you married. Or it may be you married in conscious rebellion. No matter the circumstances, God says you are married to that man and you must obey him.

But it is the wonderful providence of God that, even before we knew Him, before we were willing to yield to Him our hearts and lives, He was working to make things come out right for us. He knew what would someday be the longing of our hearts. He does not change the shape of the past; but He weaves the past with the future to make it all work out for our good, when we have turned to Him in love and let Him (Rom. 8:28).

I do not say that God will erase every penalty for thwarting His will. I do say that we can trust Him to restore the years the locusts have eaten (Joel 2:25) and to remake the marred and broken vessels for His good (Jer. 18:4), if we will let Him. Don't settle for less than God's great blessing on this home, in this place, with this man you have promised to cherish until death parts you.

But What if His Influence on the Children Is Bad?

Then make sure your influence on the children is good. Let them see a mother who loves God and keeps His commandments by obeying her husband!

Your influence, by God's grace, can counteract the bad influences a father can have. That is the meaning of

I Corinthians 7:14: "For the unbelieving husband is sanctified by the wife, and the unbelieving wife is sanctified by the husband: else were your children unclean; but now are they holy." This has been the experience of many a godly mother.

Suppose your husband gives the children permission to go to an R-rated movie. If you criticize him for it in front of the children, then you teach your children disrespect for all authority, even God's. Instead of waging a verbal battle with the father, why not talk over the movie with the children afterward? Help them to evaluate what they have seen, determine what values good or bad it taught them, and test these against the Scriptures. If you help them make decisions on the basis of what would please the Lord, then they will be making wise choices on their own. How much better that would be than to fight a battle with your husband which you cannot win without losing.

Rearing children requires a lot of faith, at best. God has given clear instructions concerning the training of children, but we fail Him so often we cannot say, "I have done every single thing about my children God told me to do." We must follow the Scriptures as closely as we are humanly able, and then we must commit our children to the hands of God to do what we are unable to do.

That's what Jochebed and Hannah both had to do. Jochebed saved her baby's life, but she didn't get to rear him. Moses grew up in the wicked, heathen court of Pharaoh, a most unlikely place for spiritual training! Yet God saw Jochebed's faith and honored it (Heb. 11:23).

Hannah did not get to rear the son God gave her after she prayed so earnestly. Samuel was raised by Eli the priest, who was a spectacular failure with his own sons (I Sam. 2). Still, "All Israel from Dan even to Beer-sheba knew that Samuel was established to be a prophet of the Lord...for the Lord revealed himself to Samuel" (I Sam. 3:20, 21). God blessed Hannah's faith and over-ruled the early influences to make him a remarkable prophet of God.

Obey God. Obey your husband. God will see to it that bad influences on the children are counteracted.

I Want to Do Right, but I Can't Help How I Feel

Carol said, "Libby, it's easy for you to obey your husband. You grew up that way. I didn't. All my life I got to do what I wanted to do. It's very hard for me to give up my own way now and obey my husband."

I could have argued with her about one thing: it isn't always easy for me to obey my husband. But I freely concede that the proper home training sure makes it easier to be an obedient wife. If you learn submission to authority as a child, it probably is less constraining to have to obey a husband when you grow up.

But that very fact makes it infinitely more important for Carol to learn to submit to her husband. Imagine the widening circle of influence. If she does not learn submission, she can't teach it to her children. They will follow her example. When they grow up, they will teach rebellion to their children. How swiftly the contamination multiplies!

No, it is now, in this generation, that Carol must break the vicious circle. She will have to claim God's grace; she will have to fight the battle of insubordination daily, perhaps hourly; but she must break the chain.

There is another aspect in the matter of submission and feelings: it is tinged with mystery. Have you noticed how many Scriptures there are that command a wife to obey her husband and how few Scriptures there are that command her to love her husband? There is only one Scripture, to my knowledge, that specifically tells a wife to love her husband, and that is Titus 2:4. Why? Because, I think, in a marvelous, supernatural way, submission brings love. If you obey him, you will love him, love him more than you ever dreamed possible.

It's a Bible principle found in Proverbs 16:3: "Commit thy works unto the Lord, and thy thoughts shall be established." You do right: you obey him, regardless of how you feel. Then your feelings turn out right—your thoughts are established. If you obey, you will love.

I am aware of the feelings of revulsion a woman may have toward her husband. They may be caused by poor teaching from childhood. They may be caused by a shattering incident in adolescence. The husband himself may not have been tender enough. But many a woman who thought she could never love the man she was bound to has discovered that, when she obeyed him, she learned to love him.

The God who made you is able to give you victory over the dark thoughts that may oppress you about this. Second Corinthians 10:5 says, "Casting down imaginations, and every high thing that exalteth itself against the knowledge of God, and bringing into captivity every thought to the obedience of Christ."

When a thought of rebellion comes, draw it out, show it to your compassionate Saviour, tell Him you cannot conquer it alone, ask Him to destroy it for you. Bring every thought into submission to Christ.

Have you come to see your need to submit? Have you asked God to help you do right in this important part of your life? Then confess it to your husband. Tell him you have been wrong, that you want him to be the head of your home. I don't promise you that suddenly everything will be sweetness and light in your home. He may test you, demand more of you than he ever has before, and make it very hard to keep your determination to obey. Bad habits are hard to break, and the way you respond to each other may be a deeply ingrained habit not easily overcome.

You will fail often. But don't quit, don't give up. Confess your rebellion to God (and to your husband, again, if need be), pick yourself up, dust yourself off, and keep trudging down the road. It may be a long road, but the joy and peace awaiting you will make it all worthwhile.

7

How to Appeal a Bad Decision

"If a woman must always obey her husband," a young wife wrote to me from California, "then you'll have to admit a woman will sometimes have to sin. I know. My husband made me get an abortion."

Another woman said, "You tell me to obey my husband, but I can't when he starts beating my son."

On another occasion a woman told me, "My husband likes to stage swinging sex parties and expects me to participate. The only way I can do that is to get drunk first. Yet you tell me to obey him!"

All three of these women were wrestling with what seems to be an irreconcilable conflict. God's Word plainly says it is wicked to murder an unborn baby. Beyond shadow of argument, it is wrong for a father to abuse a son when God has entrusted him with the duty of protecting him. It is surely sin for a man and his wife to break holy marriage vows by casual adultery.

And yet—and yet! The Scriptures do plainly tell a woman she *must* obey her husband. Now our God is holy, dependable, unchanging. Above all else, He deals with His children with integrity. That is His eternal nature. "The Lord is righteous in *all* his ways, and holy in all his works" (Ps. 145:17).

God warns us in James 1:13, "Let no man say when he is tempted, I am tempted of God: for God cannot be tempted with evil, neither tempteth he any man." God never, never sets it up so we are tempted to sin. Then how can a woman do right when her husband flatly tells her to do wrong?

Before you set out to appeal what you consider a "bad decision," ask yourself these questions to help you have the right perspective:

Am I Assuming Guilt for My Husband's Behavior?

Sometimes a wife feels torn and guilty, not because her husband asks her to do wrong, but because *he* is doing wrong. It's important to distinguish the difference. You see, God did not make a woman her husband's judge. He does not hold her accountable for her husband's actions. "The soul that sinneth, it shall die. The son shall not bear the iniquity of the father, neither shall the father bear the iniquity of the son," declares Ezekiel 18:20.

A woman can be an helpmeet and encouragement to her husband when he is beset by temptation. But if he chooses to do wrong, in spite of her love and concern, that is not her responsibility. He is accountable to God for his own decisions, his own behavior, his own sins.

Have I Consistently Obeyed Him
in the Past?

If a woman has frequently resisted her husband's authority, then she has no defense when he asks her to do wrong. That was the problem with the woman whose husband asked her to participate in his swinging sex parties.

When I asked her, "Does your husband know you really want to do right and to follow his leadership? Have you been obeying him in other areas of your life?" she gave me a withering look: "You've got to be kidding. Of course not. Why should I do what that lout says?"

"Then when he suggests a swinging sex party and you agree, though you haven't been obeying him in any other part of your life, is it because you must obey him, or because you like the idea?"

She flushed and dropped her eyes. "I see. I've been using obedience as an excuse for what I wanted to do."

God killed Sapphira along with her lying husband, not because she obeyed him, but because of her wicked collusion with him (Acts 5:1–11).

It ought never to be that your submission to your husband's authority is in question. If there has been a constant struggle in the past about who is boss, then it might well be a man would insist his wife do something truly wrong. If you question this wrong decision, he may think it's only the same old resistance, the same critical spirit, the same bad habit.

But if you have been earnestly, sweetly following his leadership, then when he asks you to do wrong, you have every right to appeal his wrong decision, as I Peter 3:4, 5 explains, without fear because you are trusting God. You have a right to appeal to God's protection so that you do not have to do wrong!

Is It Really Wrong, or Does It Just Seem Wrong to Me?

A woman in Nebraska who read this book wrote me in deep distress. She felt her husband had forced her to do wrong. They owned a wheat farm. Her husband asked her to drive a load of wheat into town to the mill to be sold. She believed that the load of wheat was too wet to sell. Her husband insisted she do it. The government wheat-buyer tested the wheat, using approved government equipment. He determined it met federal standards and bought it. Nevertheless the woman felt her husband had made her do wrong.

The problem here, it seems to me, is that the wife set herself up as the expert. She seemed to think she knew more than her husband, more than the wheat buyer, more than the government experts who set the standard and devised the testing equipment!

She would have said she had a sensitive conscience, that she earnestly wanted to please God. But she actually had a "weak" conscience, according to I Corinthians 8:7–11; and she would have done well to lean on her husband's judgment.

"The way of a fool is right in his own eyes; but he that hearkeneth unto counsel is wise," says Proverbs 12:15. "Every way of a man is right in his own eyes," warns Proverbs 21:2. So a woman ought to be careful not to assume she always is able to discern what the real right or wrong is.

King David said in Psalm 131:1, 2, "Lord, my heart is not haughty, nor mine eyes lofty: neither do I exercise myself in great matters, or in things too high for me. Surely I have behaved and quieted myself, as a child that is weaned of his mother." If the great King David had to say there were many judgments too hard for him to understand, then a woman might also sometimes have to say about a husband's decision, "I'll not be arrogant; perhaps I don't understand all that is involved here."

Can I Discover the Basic Intent of His Decision and Move to Meet That Need?

God holds a man accountable for his family. God gave him the responsibility for the long-range, eternally important decisions. Sometimes a woman will focus on the close, apparent problem; she may not see the larger issue and so not understand the basic purpose of a husband's decision.

Or perhaps she does not understand what her husband really wants from her. She hears him ask her to go to a bar with him. She thinks he is demanding she get drunk with him. But he only knows that he loves her very much and wants to be with her. He is embarrassed that she doesn't seem to like to be with him or want to meet his friends. Surely that wife could meet his God-given longing for fellowship.

Bonnie was upset with Jerry because he wanted her to go to a stock-car race with him. "Libby," she said, "how can I make him understand that I'm a Christian now and can't go to the stock-car races with him?"

I grinned at her. "Since I've never been to a stock-car race, tell me why you think you ought not to go."

"Oh, I don't like the gas-fumey atmosphere, and there's a lot of beer guzzling."

"Would Jerry expect you to drink?"

"Oh no, and he wouldn't drink either. But it's his friends—I don't think they are Christians."

"Then maybe it's time they met a good and happy Christian in you."

A little bewildered, but determined, Bonnie went with Jerry to the races. She heaped a picnic basket high with goodies. They and Jerry's friends sat down on the grass in the center of the track and had an absolutely wonderful time. And Bonnie felt it was all worthwhile when that night Jerry said, "Bonnie, I've never had a more wonderful time in my life! Thank you for being so special."

Another young wife said to me, "I can't obey my husband. He wants me to lie for him."

"About what?"

"Sometimes a customer calls the house on Saturdays, his day off, and he tells me to tell them he's not home."

"Why not simply take the message for him and tell the customer he'll contact him on Monday?"

"But I think he ought to talk to his customers."

"Then your real problem is not that your husband

is asking you to lie for him but that you feel he isn't handling his job right?"

"Well, yes, if you put it that way...I can see what you mean. He has a right not to take calls on Saturdays if he doesn't feel like it. I can handle that."

Perhaps a man asks his wife to wear clothing she believes immodest. What should she do? She needs to ask herself if she has been too constrained and inhibited in the bedroom. She needs to find ways to satisfy her husband's legitimate desire to see her body—after all, God said it belongs to him! Surely she can satisfy his needs and still dress modestly in public.

How Often Have I Tried to Convince Him Before Concerning This Course of Action?

If you have many times explained your reasons for opposing a course of action, then perhaps you ought not to say more. Sometimes I try pleading my cause with my husband one more time, speaking louder, more slowly, with more tears—and he seems to hear it as the same old argument he's already heard!

If you were not able to make your arguments reasonable and clear in earlier discussions, likely you will not be able to persuade him this time either. It's another exercise in futility and frustrating to both of you. He'll only think that you are being stubborn and won't give up, that you only want the last word.

Have you thought through clearly the reasons you oppose the decision? Are they really valid? Can you express your thoughts simply, without anger? Are you willing to bear the consequences and the burden, perhaps more than your fair share, if he should change his mind?

Is This Decision Unimportant or a Matter of Desperate, Eternal Importance?

If this decision regards something really minor, such as what color car to buy or where a picture ought to be hung, then probably a woman ought not to make a big issue of it. She ought to reserve her appeals for things that really matter to her.

At the Constitutional Convention, when our nation was founded, George Washington spoke only twice. Though he was the most beloved man in the country, he did not try to control the convention. Why didn't he speak more often? "Because, when I say something, I want people to listen."

When a wife protests a husband's decision, it ought to be so extraordinary that he will know it is important to her and so he'll listen to her.

If a family is jeopardized by serious moral or physical danger, a woman certainly should plead her cause with her husband. If he is choosing a course of action where he has shown himself especially weak, then it would be proper for a woman to express her misgivings.

About certain unassailable wrongs, a woman certainly must take her stand. She must not commit murder. She must not let her husband physically or sexually abuse the children or herself. She must not commit adultery with another man. If necessary, she must remove herself and the children from the home until the matter is properly settled or call for police protection.

Am I Using Obedience as an Excuse for Doing What I Really Want to Do but Don't Want the Responsibility For?

The young wife in California whose husband made her get an abortion perhaps fell into this trap. She said, "Why don't you admit that, if a woman must obey her husband all the time, she'll sometimes have to sin?"

She explained: "We have three children. In spite of the fact that we used contraceptives, I got pregnant again. I can't keep up with the housework. We owe lots of money. I have trouble keeping the children from quarreling. How could I handle another baby? My husband told me I had to get an abortion. I prayed that I'd lose it naturally, but I didn't, so I had to get an abortion. The next time I got pregnant, I asked God again to let me abort naturally, and I did."

This dear girl really believed that it was God's fault that she had to get an abortion in obedience to her husband! She didn't seem to realize that she'd said to her husband, in effect, "I don't want this baby any more than you do. I think God made a big mistake to let me get pregnant. If I could, I would terminate the pregnancy."

Her husband agreed with her. He didn't mind taking the blame for making her do what she really wanted to do, so he told her to go ahead and get it done.

Suppose, instead of agreeing with him that the baby was a bad mistake, that she had said, "Dear, I believe this precious little life is from God, even if we don't feel ready for it. I'm sorry that I haven't done a very good job of keeping the house clean and caring for the children. With God's help, I can fix that; and I can take care of this new baby, too. I won't complain about the sleepless nights. I'll try not to demand things we can't afford. I'll save money every way I can. I believe it would be a sin against God to murder this little baby. I beg you, please don't make me get an abortion."

If she had said that to her husband, I believe God would have put into his heart a fear of breaking His law so strong that he would have backed off from the abortion. God promised in I Corinthians 10:13 that He will always make a way to escape temptation so we won't have to sin. I believe a proper appeal would have caused that man to change his mind about the abortion.

How to Appeal a Husband's Wrong Decision

Do you have a right to appeal a bad decision? Absolutely! The Bible gives many wonderful examples of people who went to the one in authority over them to appeal what they believed to be an unfair decision. God tells us about them because He wants us to learn how to act when we find ourselves in a similar situation (because, alas, husbands, like wives, are human beings and sinners, and they will sometimes make bad decisions).

Abraham, the Old Testament patriarch, found himself in that kind of bind when he learned that God was going to destroy Sodom. Abraham went straight to God to ask how that could be. 'God, are You really going to kill all the righteous people in Sodom along with the wicked people? That's not like You. Shall not the Judge of all the earth do right?' (Gen. 18:25). Then follows one of the sweetest conversations between God and man recorded in Scripture, as Abraham persuades God to reconsider His decision!

Abraham was so committed to doing the will of God that, when God told him to offer his son as a burnt-offering, he set out to do so (Gen. 22:1-14). He didn't say, "I can't do that, God; You know that would be murder." Rather, as Hebrews 11:17-19 explains, Abraham obeyed God, thinking, *I don't understand all this, but I will do what God commands. He'll do a miracle, if necessary, and raise my son from the dead to keep His promises to me and keep me from the sin of murder.*

God always, *always* makes a "way to escape" for the child of His who obeys Him. God makes it so His children do not have to sin. So God provided Abraham a ram for the sacrifice and spared Isaac's life.

The Scriptures call Abraham "the friend of God." Perhaps he'd earned the right to argue with God. He'd proved his faithfulness in years of unflagging obedience.

But what about the half-caste Canaanite woman we're told of in the New Testament? She had a little girl tragically afflicted by demons. What right did she have to argue with God? She may have had no rights—but that didn't stop her from pleading her cause with Jesus!

She heard Jesus was in town. He'd hidden Himself in a private home and didn't want His presence to be known. He was trying to get some rest from the crowds of people who followed Him. But this Canaanite woman didn't care what Jesus wanted; she wanted her precious child healed. So she pushed her way into the house, fell at Jesus' feet, and begged Him to heal her child.

It was all pretty embarrassing—the woman tugging at Jesus' robe, His ignoring her, almost as if she weren't even there, the disciples rolling their eyes in exasperation. But she kept right on asking. Finally, the disciples said, "Lord, this woman sure is getting on our nerves. Why don't You let us send her away?"

Then Jesus broke His silence, but abruptly. "I'm sorry, Lady. I can't help you. You aren't a Jew."

But the woman wouldn't take His "no" for an answer. "Lord, help me!"

Jesus acted surprised. "Lady, I can't give the children's food to the dogs."

Undaunted, she answered, "Okay, Lord, if I'm a dog, I'm Your dog, and I need help. Please heal my daughter."

So Jesus yielded to her appeal—He'd really wanted to heal her daughter all along. Jesus, the eternal God Himself, did exactly what the poor woman asked. He healed her little girl, and she went away satisfied. You can read her story in Matthew 15:21–28 and Mark 7:24–30.

God not only "puts up with" our asking Him to change His mind; it delights Him for us to do so. As an illustration of this truth, Jesus told the parable of a judge so wicked and corrupt he didn't care what anybody—man or God—thought of him. But when a needy widow kept hounding him to rule in her favor, he finally did it. He said, "This woman is going to wear me out; I guess I'll have to change my mind." He got tired of her continual coming. If a wicked judge can be made to change his mind, Jesus said, how much more can a righteous

God be persuaded to do right (Luke 18:1-8)!

How Can I Get My Husband to Change His Mind?

The scriptural principle is stated in Proverbs 25:15: "By long forbearing is a prince persuaded, and a soft tongue breaketh the bone." The word *soft* means "tender" or "timid." God says a ruler can be persuaded to change his mind by gentle, unselfish, persistent persuasion. So a man can be persuaded to change his mind when his wife appeals in the right way.

Proverbs 15:1 says, "A soft answer turneth away wrath." The right kind of response by the one *under* authority will soften the attitude of the one *in* authority. A husband bent on a wrong course of action can be persuaded to change his mind—perhaps to his own surprise. That's the evident meaning of Proverbs 16:9: "A man's heart deviseth his way: but the Lord directeth his steps." A man might say to himself, "This is what I am going to do," but God controls what he actually does.

Ecclesiastes 10:4 says, "If the spirit of the ruler rise up against thee, leave not thy place; for yielding pacifieth great offences." Resistance to authority is not the answer when a woman feels a decision is wrong. Rather, she must appeal the decision quietly, waiting for God to work in her behalf.

This perhaps was the mistake of the woman who said she could not stand by when her husband "beat" her son. As we talked together, the mother admitted that the boy had constantly rebelled against her and defied his father. Nevertheless, she defended her son and in his presence accused the father of cruelty. But by her own description of the "beatings," it seemed to me that the father was restrained and careful in his discipline, not lashing out in anger.

The mother's possessiveness was very evident: she always referred to the child as "*my* son," not "*our* son." The father obviously was very frustrated, knowing his son desperately needed discipline; and he probably overreacted to his wife's lack of discipline. In that case, how much blame actually fell on the mother for her son's whippings? Perhaps more than she was willing to admit.

How does a woman get her husband to change his mind? Not by outrage, not by harsh words, not by threats, not by withholding her love. Rather, as I Peter 3:4 says, a woman can, by her meek (without anger) and quiet spirit (trusting God), woo her husband to do right. A godly woman obeys even an ungodly husband with the assurance that God will make his decisions turn out for good in her life.

Proverbs 16:1 says, "The preparations of the heart in man, and the answer of the tongue, is from the Lord." An absolute dictator, a king who answers to no one, cannot make decisions without God's intervention.

Proverbs 21:1 tells us, "The king's heart is in the hand of the Lord, as the rivers of water: he turneth it whithersoever he will," like the valves of an irrigation ditch turned on or off by the farmer. This Scripture does not say every decision made by every king (or any other man or woman in authority) will always be right. It does promise that God will make it turn out for good in the lives of His children who love Him and are trying to serve Him. It's the same principle as expressed in Romans 8:28: "And we know that all things work together for good to them that love God." Things not good in themselves will turn out for good for God's children!

Psalm 76:10 says of God, "Surely the wrath of man shall praise thee: and the remainder of wrath shalt thou restrain." If God cannot use an evil decision and reshape it to become a blessing to His child, then He thwarts that decision.

When God commands a woman to obey Him by obeying her husband in everything, then God takes upon Himself the responsibility to make it turn out right.

Does It Work? Does It Really Work?

A woman who came to me for counselling for her deteriorating marriage said, "Libby, I don't know what to do. I tried that 'obedience bit' and it didn't work, so now I don't know what to do."

"That obedience bit" cannot be something that you use just because it "works" and abandon when it quits "working." You obey your husband because God told you to. You obey whether it works or not.

But I tell you, on the authority of God's Word, it works. "God is not a man, that he should lie; neither the son of man, that he should repent [change his mind]: hath he said, and shall he not do it? or hath he spoken, and shall he not make it good?" (Num. 23:19). God keeps His promises. Yes, it works.

The other day my son Paul saw on my desk a booklet

I wrote, *How to Win Your Unsaved Husband.* I suppose he'd never seen it before.

"Huh—you write this?"

I nodded.

"Does it work?"

I reached for a letter that had come just that day and handed it to him. He read it out loud: "After reading *How to Win Your Unsaved Husband,* I applied the Scripture references to my life. My husband is saved now. I want to share this blessing with unequally yoked women through my testimony and give the booklet." (Signed) Mrs. K.F.P.

"Hey," Paul said, surprised, "it works!"

I get the other kind of letters, too, from women who are not about to submit to their husbands, like this one: "I do not plan to obey my husband except when it's what God wants me to do. I am told to obey God rather than man. I will go to church no matter what my husband says, because I love my Lord more than any man. If he won't get saved, he's not going to keep me from doing right."

Nearly always (I don't remember a single exception) when a woman writes that she is going to obey God instead of her husband, she has to add, "My husband is not yet saved."

It isn't coincidence. The two things are related: God has made a promise to the woman who will obey her husband. He keeps His promises. He will not honor disobedience, no matter what excuse is given for it. A woman wins her husband, draws him to a high spiritual plane, by a submissive, quiet spirit. She alienates him and dishonors the Lord if she rebels.

Yes, it really works. God will bless your home if you are obedient.

8

How to Enter In: Unconditional Surrender

The preceding pages have been written with two underlying assumptions. If I'm wrong in them, you'll think everything I have said is absolute gibberish and nonsense.

The life of obedience makes sense only if you know the Lord Jesus as your personal Saviour and if you love Him enough to be honestly willing to do whatever He commands.

If you want your way, not God's way, in your life, if you are not willing to confess your need for a Saviour, then, of course, you will not want to submit to your husband either. You may well be angry enough at me to want to burn this book!

It may be that you want to turn to Christ but do not know how. Here's what Ephesians 2:4–9 says:

"But God, who is rich in mercy, for his great love wherewith he loved us, Even when we were dead in sins, hath quickened us together with Christ, (by grace ye are

*saved;) And hath raised us up together, and made us sit
together in heavenly places in Christ Jesus. . . . For by
grace are ye saved through faith; and that not of
yourselves: it is the gift of God: Not of works, lest any
man should boast."*

This Scripture starts off by saying we were dead—
"dead in sins." Since you are alive enough to be reading
these words, it must not be talking simply about physical
death (although that is part of the penalty of sin which
you will someday pay). It is talking about spiritual death.

When we sinned against God, we forfeited our right
to get into Heaven. God is perfectly holy. He cannot let
sin contaminate Heaven. He can't overlook sin, excuse
it, and simply say, "Oh, never mind." His holiness requires that sin be paid for.

But every one of us has sinned. "For all have
sinned," Romans 3:23 says. That's where God's "rich
mercy and great love" enter in. He hates sin, but He
loves us. So Jesus paid the penalty of sin for us. He trad-
ed places with us. We were dead in our sins, so He died
in our place and gave us His righteousness.

How do you get this forgiveness? "By grace." You
can't earn it, can't deserve it. If, starting today, you lived
an absolutely sinless life, still you couldn't erase the sins
of yesterday and last week and last year. But by grace
you can be forgiven for every wicked deed, every shab-
by thought, every act of the past you've wished undone.

It is received "through faith." You do what God told
you to do—that's faith. Take Him at His word. Confess
your sins, ask Him to forgive you and make you a child

of God. Then simply believe He did what He promised you He'd do!

It seems too simple, too good to be true, but thank God it is true! You can have every sin blotted out.

I said there were two assumptions in this book: one, that you know Christ as your Saviour and, two, that you are willing to do anything God commands you to do. Unless you are willing, without any reservation of any kind, to obey Him, you will not want to obey your husband either.

Perhaps you've been afraid to tell God He can have your life as well as your heart. Perhaps you trusted Him enough to forgive you your sins but not enough to entrust your whole life to Him. You may be afraid He'd ask you to do something you've always dreaded.

Is the Holy God, who loved you so much He died for you, going to play a dirty trick on you after you surrender to Him, to make your life miserable? Never!

"What man is there of you," Matthew 7:9–11 asks, "whom if his son ask bread, will he give him a stone? Or if he ask a fish, will he give him a serpent? If ye then, being evil, know how to give good gifts unto your children, how much more shall your Father which is in heaven give good things to them that ask him?"

The loving Heavenly Father does not repay submission with rocks and scorpions! Picture yourself with your own child. Suppose he came to you and said, "Mom, I've been kinda rebellious lately, and I'm sorry. I've decided I'm going to do everything you tell me to do." After you had recovered from the shock, would you say to yourself, "Goody! I've got that brat where I want him; now what's the dirtiest thing I can make him do?"

No, no! You would be pleased and honored at his trust; you would delight in training and developing him. For his own sake, you might have to make him do an unpleasant job (because that's a part of learning to cope with life); but always he would know that you loved him and appreciated his loving trust. If we, then, being evil, give good gifts to our children—how much more shall your Father which is in Heaven?

You can trust the God who redeemed you to make the best decisions for you. This is the result promised by the familiar passage in Romans 12:1: "I beseech you therefore, brethren, by the mercies of God, that ye present your bodies a living sacrifice, holy, acceptable unto God, which is your reasonable service."

What is a sacrifice?—an animal put on the altar, slain, the blood drained out, without will or desire, to be consumed by the fires of the altar.

What is a *living* sacrifice?—a life put on the altar, with no more will or desire than a dead animal, to be consumed in the service of God, a heart attitude of absolute, unqualified surrender, to desire nothing the Lord does not desire, to feel no lack, defend no rights, expect no rewards except the joy of serving the One who gave His life for you.

People often quote Romans 12:1 and neglect the wonderful promise in verse two: ". . . that ye may prove what is that good, and acceptable, and perfect, will of God."

The will of God is good: good for you, good for those

you love, because planned by the God who loves you. It will be proven good in your life.

The will of God is perfect—perfect in its planning, perfect in its execution, perfect because planned by the God who knows everything and is able to do anything. You can prove in your life that God's will is perfect.

The will of God is acceptable. If we do His will in its goodness and perfection, then our hearts will cry out, "I delight to do thy will, O my God" (Ps. 40:8). If we will only let Him control our lives, follow His good and perfect will, then we will find it far more precious, far more satisfying than any scheme we might have foolishly devised.

The past four years our church has had a women's retreat up in the lovely foothills of the Smokies. Our women look forward to those retreats with the opportunity to get away from the cares of home for a night, talk together about mutual spiritual needs and search the Scriptures for God's answers. There's always one session around the fireplace, usually spontaneous and very late at night, when we talk together about things closest to our hearts—our homes and children, our relationships with our husbands and our God.

Each year a woman I'll call Jeanette has been there. Her husband was saved a few years ago through the ministry of the church, and they have been faithful members ever since. Jeanette would sit with us around the fireplace, listen to the discussion and (she told me later) say to herself, "It won't work. I just couldn't do that. Me, obey Walter? and him still drinking? That just won't work. I'm not going to demean myself to anybody, especially Walter."

For three years Jeanette said that. But the spiritual condition of the home deteriorated; Walter had increasing problems with alcohol; the teenage daughters got more and more rebellious. The still, quiet voice of God spoke to Jeanette's heart, saying, "Yield. Submit. Let Me take control."

Finally, in desperation, Jeanette dropped to her knees. "Dear Lord, You know I don't have it within myself to obey Walter. It's humanly impossible for me to let anybody boss me around. You will just have to take charge. I don't see how it can possibly work, but right now, I promise You, Lord, that I'll obey Walter, no matter what he says. I trust You to make it turn out right."

She said nothing of this to anyone. But at the retreat this spring, she came to the session on husband-wife relationships. Afterward she whispered, "I just had to come to this session, Libby. I didn't need it this time, thank God, but I wanted to hear it again, just to see if it would sound as ridiculous as it sounded every other year before I tried it. Sure enough, it sounded wonderful and true. It really works. I love Walter so much more than I ever loved him before. He loves me, and we have such sweet times together, even if we are old married folks! I just couldn't see how obeying him would fix all the other problems, but it did. How I wish we could have started our lives out together that way!"

Absolute, total surrender to the whole will of God! Nothing less will do. Nothing else will give you peace. Why not give back to God the ownership of your life? Why not put it all back in His loving, compassionate hands, to do whatever He deems best with it? Not until then will you find the grace to obey your husband with all your heart. Not until then will you find the satisfaction, the peace you have been seeking.

~~~ 9 ~~~

The Far-Reaching Consequences

What more is there to say?

God commands a wife to obey her husband.

He obviously meant what He said.

He made no exceptions for extenuating circumstances.

He promises guidance and wisdom to the woman who seeks to obey.

He offers unmeasured grace for whatever trials a woman faces while He completes the needed work of conviction in her husband's heart.

He rewards obedience with a usefulness and happiness far beyond her deepest expectation.

One step remains: that you take God at His Word, believe Him and obey Him by obeying your husband.

The consequences of the decision are profound—they reach across the bounds of life and death and touch eternity.

For the Sake of the Children, Submit

Children are frightened and confused by conflict in

the home. You may know that your arguments with your husband are under control, but the children don't know that. They do know families often are broken by divorce, and they have no way of knowing how that happens. They love Mother and Father both. They don't want to be forced to choose up sides one against the other. But when a mother rebels against the father's authority, the loyalties of children are bound to be divided. A child has no defense against such fears.

Nor can you be really sure that your quarrels are "under control." A girl I'll call Alice said to me, "Bud and I often argued. We both thought we could stop the argument anytime we wanted to. It was a kind of game, a serious game, but still a game. Then one day, in the heat of a quarrel, I said, 'Maybe we just ought to get a divorce.' After I said it, the words just hung in the air between us. Until that day neither one of us intended to break up our home. But after that, it was downhill all the way. Now here I am—left with these three children to raise alone."

No, quarrels between a husband and wife, like small campfires in the forest, can suddenly rage out of control. In any unresolved conflict between husband and wife, there is always great danger to the marriage, however trivial its beginning. Children instinctively know the sanctity of the home itself is endangered when there is conflict over who is boss.

Not only will the children suffer from fear, they will also learn from a rebellious mother her rebellion against authority. (I'm sure it's more contagious than the black plague! How many times have I heard my own grumblings echoed back to me in the whining voices of my children!) The children will learn rebellion and rebel against you and your husband. Then they will resent all authority: the school, the boss, the policeman, the structure of life itself. The end of the road of rebellion is sure heartache.

You don't need to fear that your obedience will lessen your children's respect for you. When you set the standard by your obedience, you can require the same obedience from them. The command, "Honour thy father and thy mother" (Exod. 20:12), shows God requires the child to obey father and mother equally. He is to obey his mother exactly as he obeys his father—that's the chain of command. When a mother obeys her husband, she enhances her own authority with the child rather than diminishing it.

If you love your children, if you covet their future happiness and usefulness, make sure they have a mother who submits to her husband.

For Your Husband's Sake, Obey

Friction between husband and wife is a terrible consumer of energy. It drains the body of drive, wastes the resources of the mind, dissipates the usefulness of emotion, and consumes enormous amounts of time. Talk about wasted resources! Surely conflict in the home is one of the greatest of wastes!

Think of the creative work a man can do, secure in the knowledge that his wife loves him, trusts his decisions, works by his side, not against him. That man can give himself wholeheartedly to the task at hand and not fritter away the time fighting (or yielding to) nagging doubts and fears.

Imagine how quickly a man would turn his steps homeward in the evening, after a day of grappling with the world, if the woman who waited for him met him with words of tenderness on her lips instead of a set of ultimatums. Then there would be no need for the defenses a man sometimes uses—the briefcase full of office work, the newspaper attentively read, the television left on full blast the whole evening. Then there would be plenty of time for talking and communing, plenty of energy for sharing and loving. A man so loved and so sustained would face the world the next day with zest and courage and likely be successful in the work he attempted.

If it matters at all to you about the man you have promised to love until parted by death, for his well-being and joy, for his usefulness to God, obey him!

For Your Own Welfare and Happiness, Yield

There's a strange paradox in Scripture, echoed in many places: if you would live, you must die (John 12:24). If you would keep your life, you must lose it (Matt. 10:39). If you would be free, you must submit yourself a slave to Christ (Rom. 6:18). And there is one more paradox which must be taken by faith as well: if you would know true freedom, you must submit to your husband's authority. Obedience certainly has its final great reward in Heaven, but it also has the present tangible reward.

"If ye keep my commandments," Jesus said, "ye

shall abide in my love. . . . These things have I spoken
unto you, that my joy might remain in you, and that
your joy might be full" (John 15:10, 11). Full joy comes
by keeping the commands of the Lord Jesus! Proverbs
29:18 promises: "He that keepeth the law, happy is he."
John 13:17: "If ye know these things, happy are ye if
ye do them." Obedience brings happiness.

Evidently a woman's submission to her husband
liberates her from a multitude of frustrating, binding
problems and conflicts. Her obedience frees her to become a whole woman and lets her use to the ultimate
every gift she has of wisdom and inventiveness and love.
Just because she is obedient does not mean she is limited
only to the interests that traditionally have been feminine. It will include cooking, clothing, housekeeping and
child-tending, of course, because those are an essential
part of being a wife and mother. But within the frame-
work of her husband's authority, she may follow any in-
clination in her leisure time: welding sculptures or tun-
ing up an automobile motor or following major league
baseball or trout casting. (Don't laugh—I know some truly feminine women who enjoy these traditionally male
interests with the amused forbearance of their spouses!)

She may find fulfillment in baking bread or concoct-
ing fancy desserts or making hooked rugs. She may find
it, as one of my friends does, in running an offset print-
ing press in her home and mailing newsletters for missionaries. She may paint portraits or paint the house.
She may raise beagles or begonias, chase butterflies or
follow the stock market. She is not confined to a nar-
row, dull range of activity simply because she obeys her

husband. There is no single description of a woman who, honoring her husband, still finds a whole wide world outside, created by God to be explored and enjoyed. And she savors it to the full.

But it is not for the trifles, the amusements, the "toys" a doting husband might permit, that the intelligent, spiritually minded woman wants freedom. She wants to "be somebody" in her own right! She wants it to make a difference that she lived and worked and died. She wants to accomplish something tangible and helpful for this battered old world so full of human tragedy.

It is a blessed fact that this, too, is available to the woman who honors and obeys her husband. I don't promise you can be a famous trial lawyer or the doctor who discovers the cure for cancer or author of the great American novel or prima donna of the Metropolitan Opera. (It's conceivable that a woman with talent could do these and still be an obedient wife.) I do promise that, if you use God's standard to measure what is great and important, your individual, private life can be highly successful.

Of course God's standard of success is not the same as the world's standard—not fame or wealth or social position. He says in II Corinthians 4:18, "The things which are seen are temporal [temporary]; but the things which are not seen are eternal." If it will last forever, then it is not tangible—it cannot be touched with the hand or measured on a chart. Who but God could measure the abiding influence a godly mother has in the lives of her children day by day, patiently molding their character? How can we tell what great influence a woman can have on a confused and burdened friend as she offers a hot cup of coffee and a quiet word of help? Who can possibly know how much a wife's prayers and encouragement increase a man's productivity to God?

If it is people, not things, which are important in God's sight (and it is), then a woman can accomplish eternal good. The editor of the local paper may never hear her name, but up in Heaven the God who sees all and who cares about faithful service in lowly tasks will see and keep the record and someday reward. Matthew 10:42 tells us He rewards even the gift of a cup of cold water. Daniel 12:3 says, "And they that be wise shall shine as the brightness of the firmament; and they that turn many to righteousness as the stars for ever and ever."

Furthermore, the woman who submits to her husband will share a oneness with him, a communion she never dreamed of, an emotional peace and security positively unattainable when she struggles with him for power in the home.

It is simply not possible for a woman to wage a sparring bout all day long with her husband and then to expect, when the light is turned off in the bedroom at night, that the built-up animosity can be turned off as easily. If a woman has thwarted her husband's will during the day and jockeyed for advantage, she will not find he feels especially tender and loving at night. Mutual physical need may drive a couple through the motions of love; but she will feel frustrated and misused, a "sex object" rather than a wife; and he will wonder, in shame, what makes the whole business seem so sordid and tasteless.

God intended the union of man and wife to be inexpressibly sweet, satisfying beyond words. But the entering into that garden of mystery and wonder is through the door of a wife's submission. There is great joy beyond that gate! For your own sake, enter in.

There is another important, very personal reason why a woman ought to obey her husband, and that is for her own spiritual welfare. There is nothing so shattering as to need desperately God's help and not be able to reach Him. Yet this is the consequence of disobedience.

"Behold, the Lord's hand is not shortened," Isaiah 59:1, 2 says, "that it cannot save; neither his ear heavy, that it cannot hear: But your iniquities have separated between you and your God, and your sins have hid his face from you, that he will not hear." If you would have God's blessing on your life, if you want Him to listen when you pray, if you want His smile of approval, then don't let the sin of rebellion stand unchallenged in your life!

You may decide, having weighed all the consequences, that you want your own way, that you have rights, and that you intend to keep them. Your rights will make a very poor companion for the lonely years that lie ahead. Can they make up for the sense of unfulfillment, the frustration of plans, the dim realization of a stunted personality?

You may decide to yield. Oh, if only you will yield, what joy and peace with God lie ahead! What usefulness and fruitfulness in the home and in the community you will experience for the Lord! What personal joy and fellowship you will have with your husband...

...If only you will yield!

. . . .

Some years ago in a church service my husband and I heard missionaries request prayer for a home for their fourteen-year-old daughter. They felt it necessary to leave Polly in the States during this term of service so she could get a good education. The Lord worked it out so that Polly could live with us for the next three years.

Then her parents came home, the family moved far away, so we never saw her again though we corresponded occasionally. Polly married as soon as she graduated from high school. The babies came one after another in rapid succession until there were six.

In March of this year, Polly wrote to say that her husband David, only thirty-three years old, had died suddenly of a heart attack. To help her children overcome their sorrow, she was going to take them on a camping trip south for the summer. They would spend a week with us, if it suited our schedule, within a few weeks. Of course it suited our schedule. I would have stayed home from a round-the-world cruise to get to see Polly again!

Late one night after the thirteen children (my seven, her six) had all been tucked into bed, we poured ourselves a cup of coffee at the kitchen table. Polly told me then of the years God gave her with David.

They had been very happy in their early years of

marriage, attended church together and served the Lord. But when the babies started coming, David had to take on a second job. Polly's pregnancies were difficult, full of emergencies that endangered her life and the babies. There was a misunderstanding at the church they attended, so they decided to attend elsewhere. But since David worked on Sundays and since Polly was ill so often, it was difficult to find another church. They drifted away from the Lord, not intentionally and not perceptibly. But soon there was no spiritual life at all in the home.

Of course they weren't happy about it. But Polly would say to herself, "It's humanly impossible for me to get three children ready for church all by myself. If David helped me, I'd barely make it, but by myself? Never!... Besides, it's his responsibility to find a church."

But the Holy Spirit continued to convict Polly. Under His gentle probing, she began to realize that, whatever David's spiritual condition, she could not continue to ignore her own spiritual needs. She said ruefully that night over the cup of coffee, "So I took myself in hand. I decided I would serve the Lord no matter how hard it was."

It was hard, but she went to church. She saw that the children were dressed and ready on time. She assumed the leadership of a girls' weekday group. She spent more and more time at church.

But David, rather than being happy about it, began to complain. On Sunday mornings he would get up right at 9:30, just as Polly was getting the children into the

car to leave for Sunday school, and demand his
breakfast! Polly's first reaction (as mine would have
been) was to blow up and indignantly refuse. But the
Holy Spirit reminded her that the way to reach David
was not to rebel but to obey. Then she planned her Sunday mornings so that she fixed David's breakfast, load-
ed the children in the car, and then came back to the
house for a quick cup of coffee with him before she left
for church. She dropped some of her church commitments
and concentrated on being the wife David wanted her
to be.

Three years went by. David often seemed harder to
please than in the old days when they both were away
from the Lord. But Polly quietly and meekly obeyed him,
doing as carefully as she knew how what the Lord commanded. Then came the day (Polly's brown eyes sparkled
with tears as she told this) when David did acknowledge
his backsliding. He turned back to the Lord with all his
heart. He assumed the spiritual leadership of the home.
He found a good, Bible-believing church, and the family entered into its ministry wholeheartedly.

What a happy time they now experienced together!
Because the house was full of children, David regular-
ly got up an hour earlier than anyone else to meet the
Lord face to face without interruption. Evenings, after
the children were in bed, he and Polly fellowshipped
together in the Scriptures. Their lives bore much fruit.

Three years more went by. David and Polly were
asked to sponsor the young people's work at the church.
It was not a light task, and they were greatly exercised
as to what the will of God might be. That night they

sought clear leading from God. He seemed to lead them to Colossians, chapter 1, where they read that they should wait with patience until the time He would show them exactly what to do. Secure in the close sense of God's direction and presence, they went to sleep.

The next morning, as was his custom, David got up for his Bible reading. An hour later, when Polly got up, she found him dead.

"Oh, Libby," Polly said, her voice breaking with emotion, "what if I hadn't paid the price? What if I hadn't been willing to obey him wholly all those months? Just think! We wouldn't have had those three blessed years together! And if we hadn't had that, I don't think I could bear his being gone now!"

But she had been willing to obey, and the Lord rewarded her faithfulness in a way so marvelous she could not have anticipated it.

. . . .

Do you remember, I wonder, that day—how long ago was it?— when you first realized how much you love the man you married? Can you remember the wonder of it all, the awe, the delight you felt in his presence? Remember how you felt that, if you had him, you could put your hand in his and without a backward glance of regret, leave it all behind and walk with him, hand in hand, anywhere in the whole wide world without fear?

He is still that same man. Can you not love him enough, trust him enough, and trust God enough to give back to him that sweet, simple faith in his ability to love you and make the decisions that will make you happy?

It's there, all there, a marvelous world of love and trust and usefulness to him and God, all waiting for you to claim through the simple act of submission.

For a complete list of books available from the Sword of the Lord, write to Sword of the Lord Publishers, P. O. Box 1099, Murfreesboro, Tennessee 37133.